THE FACE OF FOLK MUSIC

Mississippi John Hurt, 1964

THE FACE

photographs by DAVID GAHR
text by ROBERT SHELTON

OF FOLK MUSIC

THE CITADEL PRESS   *NEW YORK*

First Edition

Copyright © 1968 by David Gahr and Robert Shelton

All rights reserved

Published by Citadel Press, Inc., 222 Park Avenue South,
New York, N.Y. 10003. Published simultaneously in Canada
by George J. McLeod Limited, 73 Bathurst St., Toronto 2B,
Ont. Printed by Reehl Litho., Inc., New York, N.Y. Bound
by The Haddon Craftsmen, Inc., Scranton, Pa.

Designed by A. Christopher Simon

Library of Congress catalog card number: 67-25657

For Ruth, Carla and Seth, with love,
                                        D.

*My deep apologies to the hundreds of folksingers
left unphotographed on the coming pages.*

CONTENTS

I	PAST MEMORIES, FUTURE VISIONS	1
II	ROOTS DEEP IN THE COUNTRY	39
III	EARLIER FOLK REVIVALS	73
IV	THE BIG REVIVAL, 1958 TO TOMORROW	107
V	A SONG OF PRAISE, AND A SONG OF FREEDOM	169
VI	BIG SOUND FROM THE COUNTRY	199
VII	THE MANY FACES OF THE BLUES	229
VIII	A RIVER WITHOUT END	285
	INDEX	367

THE FACE OF FOLK MUSIC

Concert of religious
music Sunday at Newport, 1964

I PAST

MEMORIES, FUTURE VISIONS

Call this a memory book, a family album of American folk music. Call it, perhaps, a prologue to the future, for it is meant to be all these things. David Gahr's camera eye is here to guide you, entice you, remind you, and move you.

His camera was able to stop time for a fraction of a second, just long enough to record the expression on the face of a singer, the aura of an audience, the ambience of a particular place and time. The artistry of the photographer will, we hope, almost make you "hear" the photograph.

To this museum on film let me add a few of my own verbal photographs. So much has happened in these ten years of the big folk revival that it could take ten books to retell it all. I'll just put my memory snapshots beside the photographs of David Gahr and hope the composite will help you remember an era.

The face of folk music is complex. It is the heavy lines that etch the years of Mississippi John Hurt in bronze. It is the long, free-flowing hair of Joan Baez. It is the puckishness of Jack Elliott, the cool aloofness of Bill Monroe, the quiet dignity of Judy Collins.

2

1966

Buffy Sainte-Marie and Jimmy Driftwood, 1966

Also—an important also—the face of folk music is the myriad face of an audience. Being an involvement art, not a spectator sport, folk song always puts the listener into the picture. So here are you or your brother and sisters or children or parents growing up in the 1960's, to the accompaniment of a six-string guitar and a five-string banjo.

Before this decade, too many persons felt that folk music was a very, very simple matter. They thought of the simplest of ditties—"Froggie Went A-Courting" or "I Gave My Love a Cherry." The closer you get to the face of folk music and the heart of folk music the more complexity there is behind the simple façade. It is, has been, and will continue to be a rather complicated, highly variegated form of artistic expression. Froggy may have gone a-courting, but he came back with such other things on his mind as romantic rebellion, the struggle for individuality, the attempt to tell the machines: "Don't fold, spindle or mutilate me, brother."

Today, folk music is as much a part of popular music in America as it has been in the countries of Latin America, Asia, and Europe for centuries. It took this final ten-year push to establish that fact. There had been folk-song lovers and practitioners since "good old colony days," but never has folk song held such mass sway as it does today.

Go to any college campus and you will find a hive of balladeers and guitar-pickers. Scratch the surface of any big city and you will find a few dozen persons here, a score there, who know that Bluegrass is rural jazz, who think that Child ballads rank with the gems of poetic expression in our language.

It is easy, much too easy, to sermonize about the folk movement and to sloganize about its brotherhood and good fellowship. That is part of the movement, to be sure, but perhaps the slogans have been too facile, the sermons too preachy. Instead, I prefer to broach the question: How did a sophisticated city girl like Joan Baez meet a back-country herdsman-songster like John Hurt?

The answer to that question, I submit, is the answer to the essential magic element of folk music. We've known about music as an international art for centuries, but has any music so united such people of different backgrounds, social milieus, and contexts before? I think not. City people learned from country people during this folk revival, and the learning process is still going on. And it is the most painless learning process imaginable, because it is out of the classroom and into the real world. Because it is fun and pleasure almost all the way.

Not everyone kept his sense of humor in these last ten years. Quite a few of us began to

Mrs. Mitch Greenhill and Jack Elliott, 1966

4

think it was all a big business. Quite a few of us got to preaching sermons on the mount when we should have been down in the valley having more fun. The intellectualization of a musical movement can often stultify its free growth, just as the anti-intellectualization of a movement can root it all in illogical feeling. Somewhere, the very rules of music—from the back porch to the conservatory—were the only rules that helped keep things on the right track: harmony, balance, proportion, staying in tune.

Withal, there were times when the folk movement nearly betrayed itself. When an audience at the Newport Folk Festival of 1965 booed and shouted at Bob Dylan, we realized that something had gone wrong, that we had lost our sense of humor and our sense of tolerance. It was a bit like the excesses of the Colonial Puritans, refugees themselves from religious persecution become bigoted in their new ascendancy.

I'll talk, in these essays, about some of the high points in the history of American folk performance. But I'll also dwell on some of the low points, because I think we all tend too much to ignore our faults. David Gahr kept his camera out of dark places, but I'll poke around there a bit to scare out the bats.

But don't let this dissuade you from feeling that this revival has been worth it, for it certainly has. There have been so many shining

Elizabeth Cotten, 1964

moments of sheer glory: The revelation of Joseph Spence's turbulent guitar-picking; the keening voice of Skip James; the everyone-singing-together at a Pete Seeger concert, the quiet explorations of four musical cultures by Sandy Bull at Indian Neck; the super-heat of The Staple Singers at the University of Chicago; the mad fiddling at Union Grove; the electric moments at Newport when the whole world seemed together for a moment; the nights of jam-sessions in the Viking Hotel after the big Newport concerts; the awesome quiet and repose in Manhattan's Gaslight when a performer was really holding his audience; the first thrills of getting space in national magazines for the folk world after so many years; the unfamiliarity with TV cameras, at first; the sheer flood of recordings and books and song-sheets and folios and instrument-methods; the guest appearances on small radio stations; Joan and Bobby singing "With God on Our Side" together; Ralph Rinzler's

Cape Breton Singers, 1965

Mike Seeger and Roscoe Holcomb, 1965

boundless enthusiasm for the latest in his dozens of rural discoveries; Archie Green telling the audience of The New York Folk Festival, "Chuck Berry's ballet turned me on, but so does the singing of Sarah Gunning." The list of high points would fill many pages.

The low points would fill a few lines. Mostly, they stemmed from the backlash of The Beatles and the emergence of Bob Dylan's new turn of the road, folk-rock. Where the purist folk fan had felt that pop-

Janis Joplin, 1968

Pete Seeger and Newport Children's Folk Festival, 1966

9

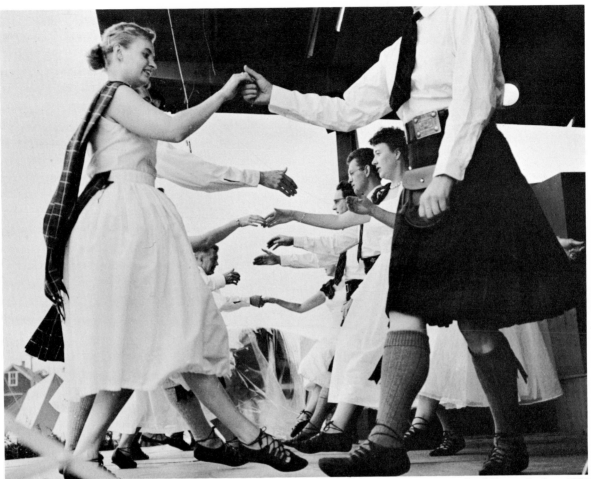

New England Dance Society, 1959

folk, á la The Limeliters, was rather thin, almost insipid, the purists fell apart at the conceivable complexity of folk-rock. But the years have passed, and the split has mostly been healed. Even Pete Seeger has recorded with the electric guitars of The Blues Project now, and we may even look forward to the possibility of hearing such bands of the future as Irwin Silber and The Dogmatists or Izzy Young and The Johnny-Come-Latelies.

Perhaps the very lowest point was hit with the New York Folk Festival, when an outsider, Manny Fox, thought he could put on an esthetically strong set of Carnegie Hall programs. But the New York Folk Festival showed too much of the rivalries and jealousies in the folk establishment of those who

should have extended their help and experience, but rather let the festival go on to its financial failure and esthetic triumphs.

Still, on balance, the good times are the ones we remember most. And the good times are still with us. Not every young singer or instrumentalist can look toward making a good living in folk song every day, nor can obscure country people think they will find fame and fortune with city audiences. But the core of substance remains untrammeled, and the audience is just about the most knowledgeable audience in the world.

Much remains to be done, for there are a lot of doors that haven't yet been opened. A lot of the excellent journalism of folk music was self-taught and learned by such people as

10

Newport, 1966

Newport, 1963

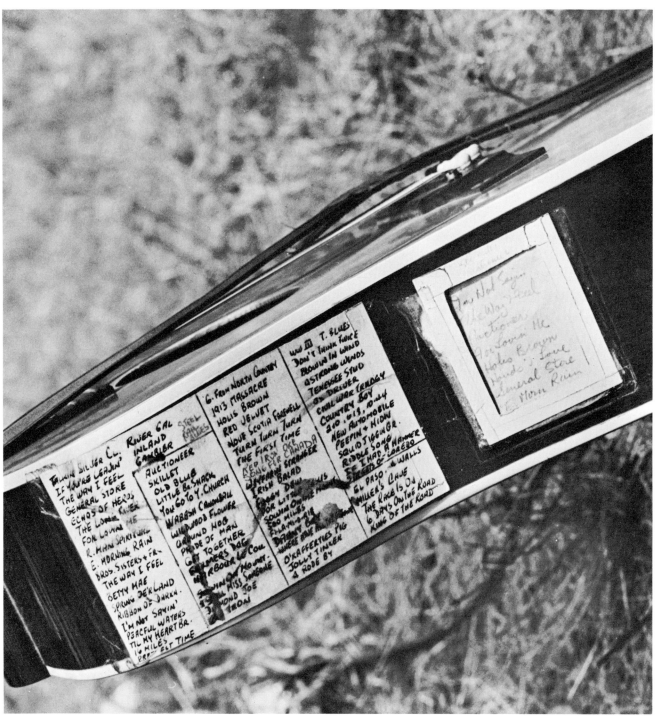

Gordon Lightfoot's guitar, 1965

Alan Lomax, 1964

(*Opposite page*) Mimi and Dick Fariña playing before crowd,
at the Newport Folk Festival, July 1965

John Hartford, 1968

Negro Religious Song at Newport Folk Festival, 1966

Cajun Band, 1965

(Top) Jean Ritchie and Seamus Ennis, 1964,
(Bottom) Linda Solomon and Seamus Ennis

B. B. King, 1968

Bob Davenport
and Clarence Ashley, 1963

1966

1966

Michael Cooney, 1968

Buell Kazee, 1968

Solomon of the Kaleidoscope, 1968

Buddy Guy and Junior Wells, 1968

Rev. Frederick Kirkpatrick, 1968

Folk audience, 1964

Roy Acuff

A. L. Lloyd
and Mary Travers, 1965

Newport, 1960

22

George Hamilton IV, 1968

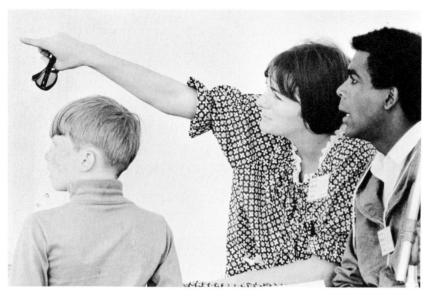

Clark Taylor, Judy Collins, and Bill Lee, 1966

1966

23

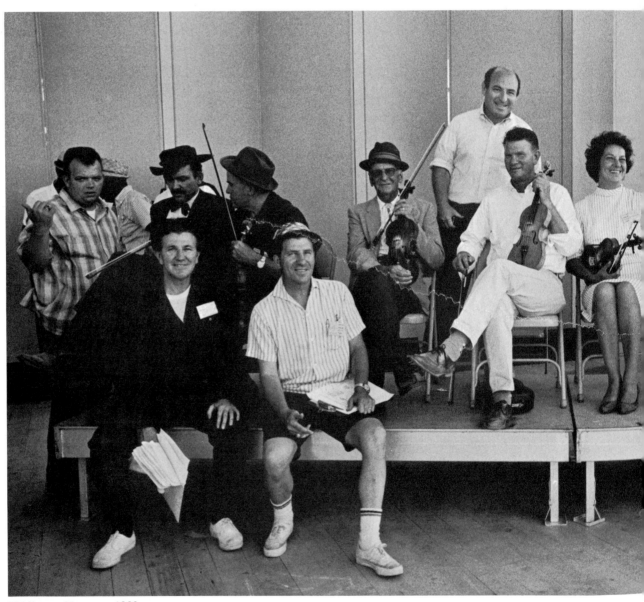

Fiddlers at Newport, 1966

Minneapolis's Paul Nelson of *The Little Sand Review* and Dave Wilson of *Boston Broadside*. But, from the standpoint of professional journalism, the folk field remains generally mired in subjective amateurism. In general terms, too many folk devotees are more hung up on country expeditions than they are in discovering folk traditions down the street in their own cities and towns. The use of folk music in film and television is in a still-primitive stage, and the use of the sound-film for total field collecting is still in its infancy.

All of this lies ahead, as does the ultimate problem of developing leadership in this movement. The Newport Folk Foundation has done much to reduce the anarchy in the folk movement, but this, too, must improve.

Taj Mahal, 1968

Janis Ian, 1968

1966

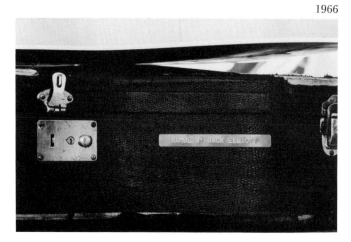

Folk audience

Sally Angie, 1968

Toshi and Pete Seeger, 1966

Newport, 1964

Newport, 1965

1964

28

Cajun Band, 1966

The feet of Glenn Ohrlin, 1964

Sean Gagnier and Bruce Murdoch, 1968

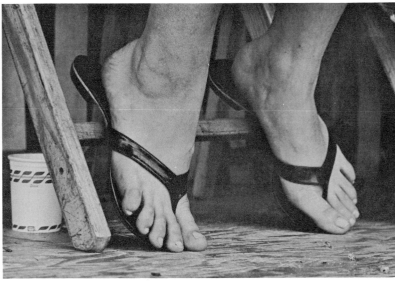

The feet of Mary Travers, 1964

Some of the best things in folk song have been achieved with spontaneity, and perhaps the old-timers who still believe that is the only way for things to develop may be right. If that be the case, we can hope only for a little better planned spontaneity in all the various media in which folk song is so applicable and flexibility available.

So, here is our memory book of pictures, with a few additional lyrics. We hope these pages sing to you and come alive in either your imagination or your memory. This is "how it was" for the last ten years. We'll let *you* write, photograph, and sing the way it will be for the next ten.

The hands of Margaret Barry, 1965

Newport Folk Festival, 1964

Children's dances
and folksinging at
Newport Folk Festi-
val, 1966

Members of the Landreneau Cajun Band, with Ian and
Sylvia Tyson and Gordon Lightfoot, 1965

Onward Brass Band, 1968

Fannie Lou Hamer (Negro Religious Song), 1966

A. L. Lloyd, Michael Gorman, Margaret Barry, Annie
Walters, and Arthur Nicolle, 1965

34

Dan Smith, 1968

II   ROOTS

DEEP IN THE COUNTRY

There was clearly something wrong with American youth in the late 1950's. Earnest debates were being held about national purpose by some of the American leaders who had not been able to articulate a national purpose in their long public careers. It was still the backwash of the McCarthy Era, the left-over time of "The Silent Generation."

How did "The Silent Generation" become "The Singing Generation"? Mostly, it was through a search for a better set of values than they were finding in the college classroom, the

advertising boardroom, the beatnik bars and coffeehouses of the mid-1950's. Jack Kerouac and his coterie were trying to say something that diagnosed the ills of America, but the solution of the Beats was too vague, too chancey, too personal, and too escapist to form a mass movement. The folk revival offered something that promised to be considerably more wholesome and constructive.

What the folk revivalists were saying, in effect, was: "There's another way out of the dilemma of modern urban society that will

teach us all about who we are. There are beautiful, simple, relatively uncomplicated people living in the country, close to the soil, who have their own identities, their own backgrounds. They know who they are, and they know what their culture is because they make it themselves: in their whittling, their embroidery, their painting, but mostly in their singing. Look to the country, confused city boy, and you will find yourself again."

It was romanticism of the first degree, as romantic as Wordsworth's rejection of Lon-

don for the lake country of England, as romantic as Rousseau's espousal of "the noble savage," as romantic as Gauguin's flight to the South Pacific. Traditionally, in times of stress, the victim of over-civilization finds himself rejecting the civilization and looking for simple truths, for the seemingly uncomplicated fusion of life, thought, and action that the "primitive" enjoys.

Needless to say, this was one of the oversimplifications of all romantic flight back to the soil. Inevitably, they would find that the "untouched" or uncorrupted simple man no longer existed on this globe. Often, there was disillusionment, too, at finding that things were not all that simple, that poverty brought its own special breed of despair, that there was narrowness and fear and xenophobia.

But the positive merits of rediscovering simplicity seemed to far outweigh the occasional disillusion. It seemed mostly like a great adventure, to leave concrete streets and concrete jails and to find, or look for, at least, the frontier of America's ethos. Long before the Kennedy Administration posited the slogan, "The New Frontier," the folk revivalists were exploring their own new frontier, traveling to the country, in actuality or in imagination, trying to find out if there was truly a more exciting life in America's continuing past.

The rediscovery of our folk roots and traditions took several forms. First, there were collecting expeditions in great number. The invention of the tape recorder had made this economically feasible, and everyone became his own Cecil Sharp or John Lomax, living the life of the ballad-hunter. It was the adventure of filling in missing links, seeking out lost persons, filling gaps in stories, concretizing living legends, pursuing myths to their sources. We had a small army then of field collectors spinning out into the Southern Appalachians, for this area seemed to be the absolute height, figuratively and literally, of rural romanticism.

Then recordings began to appear in great numbers. Folkways, Riverside, Prestige, Folk-Lyric, Elektra, and Folk-Legacy, were the main trappers of the magic rural moment. Field re-

1955

42

cordings enjoyed an enormous vogue, where once they had seemed only an expedient for getting authenticity, now they were recognized as infinitely more realistic than any studio session could be. A few collectors began to work with still camera as well as tape recorder, but the ultimate collector's tool, the sound camera, was slow to arrive.

Another step was to attend to the old-time fiddlers' conventions. Some went to Warrenton, Virginia, only to be discouraged at the number of commercial country and rock 'n' roll musicians there. Others went to Galax, Virginia, where local rules banned any electric instruments. Other citybillies went where Pete Seeger had ventured back in the mid-1930's, to the Asheville Folk Festivals of Bas-

colm Lamar Lunsford, the minstrel of the Appalachians.

An old-time fiddlers' convention that seemed to embody most of the best elements and excitement of a rural folk festival was in Union Grove, North Carolina. I recall vividly the surprises and pleasures of journeying to the Union Grove Fiddlers' Convention in spring, 1961, with Bob Yellin of The Greenbriar Boys and Charles Rothschild, a personal and concert manager. It was near the beginning of a long and rewarding interchange and dialogue for this city sophsiticate with country people.

Beyond the chance to hear a weekend of exceedingly diverse folk-rooted country music, it was a chance to get to know people from a

Robert Pete Williams and Hobart Smith, 1964

basically agrarian society, only slightly changed by the modern world. True, they did watch TV, see movies, and read the AP news reports. Yet these people were as far apart in style and life-aspirations from the three city visitors as imaginable.

We were greeted with the sort of warmth that is legendary for the South, and generally treated as honored guests. There was some surprise and considerable feelings of flattery that the music these people had been making for so long was becoming popular among city and college audiences. They weren't quite sure why, but they had always thought the music was the best in the world, so why not? Bob Yellin was honored with a special prize

Butch Cage, Harry Oster, and Willie Thomas, 1960

Almeda Riddle, 1964

Sam McGee, 1965

Horton Barker, 1965

for his fine Bluegrass banjo-picking, as still another token of reciprocal friendship. The city turn-out for such annual events as the Union Grove Convention grew steadily during the 1960's until there were perhaps two hundred New Yorkers making expeditions.

After occasional forays into the country to tape and interview country musicians or visits to various rural festivals, the city folk enthusiasts then began to do their collecting on a deeper level—they began to "collect the musicians," cultivate the friendships of the rural musician they found and become their sponsors, to see that they would get work along the folk concert circuit.

Thus did Mike Seeger sponsor The Stanley Brothers, Ralph Rinzler squire Bill Monroe and Doc Watson, John Cohen become Roscoe Holcomb's patron and good friend. The list grew and grew, with an especial pride being shown by each of the citybillies with his new-found hill country friend. This true collecting ran counter to some earlier work by folklorists who had tended, in their pressured haste or varied goals, to, in the words of one source singer, the highly perceptive blind Virginian, Horton Barker, "milk the cow dry and throw the empty hide away."

Whatever past crimes or discourtesies had been committed by earlier collectors toward their singers, the young collectors of the current folk revival went to the opposite extreme. They were treating their country friends not so much as curiosities or finds, but as cherished friends, and no one could intrude on this sort of relationship.

Through such groups as the Friends of Old-Time Music and the Newport Folk Festival, the country was brought to the city. Not always did it mean as great or as relaxed or meaningful a performance on stage as on a back porch. But the efforts—and the achievements of this transplanting were great. In Greenwich Village, in one season, a city folk fan could hear, see, and ultimately meet a whole range of ethnic stars—Doc Watson, Tom Ashley, Maybelle Carter, Horton Barker, Almeida Riddle, and on and on. At a blues concert at New York University, the

Sara Gunning, 1964

46

Big Bill Broonzy, 1958

Kirk and Sam McGee, 1965

Clark Kessinger (Seated), 1966

Moe Asch, Sonny Terry,
and Brownie McGhee, 1958

Mance Lipscomb, 1965

Kirby Snow, 1966

John Lee Hooker, 1963

Maybelle Carter, 1963

Paul Cadwell, 1964

Eck Robertson, 1965

Larry Older, Roscoe Holcomb, and Fiddler Bob Beers, 1965

Sara Carter, 1967

Jean Ritchie *(Face hidden)*, Roscoe Holcomb, and Beth Van Over, 1965

Roscoe Holcomb, 1965

Almeda Riddle and Hobart Smith, 1964

Hobart Smith, 1964

Grant Rogers, 1966

blues collector Sam Charters introduced such historically important stylists as Gus Cannon, Furry Lewis, and Memphis Willie Borum. That historic concert impelled this commentator to write:

"We read James Baldwin to get an insight into the thinking and emotion of the Southern Negro. But this concert raised a question for one listener: Do we read too much by intellectuals and listen too little to the joys and the troubles of the 'unlettered' as they express themselves in their blues songs? It is not an easy message to listen to, but it is an important one."

As time passed and we all became increasingly familiar with true rural style, mountain or blues, white and Negro, we found that it was a language of music that made complete sense, technically as well as emotionally. We got to know what the late Frank Proffitt meant when he sang his famed "Tom Dooley" song and banged his old fretless banjo. We sensed the inherent tragedy in the fact that Sam and Kirk McGee were lionized in the North and just sort of kept aboard "Grand

49

Mississippi John Hurt, 1963

Ole Opry" for tradition's sake. We got to know more members of The Ritchie Family than the lovely Jean, who had already done so much to help us understand what a singing family's life was like in the Cumberland Mountains.

There were attendant changes in the singers. No one exactly went "commercial" as they tend to do in Nashville, but they began to make clear-cut professional plans, realizing that there was an audience, an undreamed of audience, for their "home music," their back-porch music. This lionization by the folk audience startled and delighted the rural people. In some instances it brought them the money and recognition they had been denied for a lifetime. In most instances it gave them something equally important—the chance to speak their minds, to "sing their minds," for hundreds and thousands of enthusiastic young people. This aspect of the folk revival was one of its wonders.

One of the newly rediscovered "ethnic stars" who was taken to the heart of the folk revivalists was Mississippi John Hurt. His story was typical of the revolution in personal lives brought on by the folk revival. Mississippi John had been presumed dead by the collectors of his 1928 recordings until his rediscovery in March, 1961. Found in his home hamlet of Avalon, Mississippi, John Hurt was to be moved with awesome speed to a national prominence that baffled him as much as it delighted him.

At 72, John Hurt was a country blues man and songster of compelling artistry. Far from being the "primitive" music-maker one might have expected to find in the hills at the edge of the Mississippi Delta, Mr. Hurt was a weaver of subtle, complex sounds. His per-

Mississippi John Hurt and Dorsey Dixon, 1963

Mississippi John Hurt and Sleepy John Estes, 1964

Sleepy John Estes, 1964

Robert Wilkins, Gaither Carlton, Skip James, Arnold Watson, Mississippi John Hurt, Yank Rachel, Sleepy John Estes, Hammy Nixon, and Doc Watson, 1964

formances had the quiet, introspective quality of chamber music. Mississippi John made an unforgettable visual impact. He was a short, stoop-shouldered former railroad-gang worker, cattle herdsman, and farmer. His face was a study in corrugated bronze. Deep furrows between his eyes pointed down a large nose to a strong, projecting jaw, where two crescent creases seemed to place the singer's

mouth between parentheses. Pulled down to his ears was his trademark, a stained brown round-brimmed felt hat, which Mississippi John had bought six years earlier from a mail-order catalogue.

He tuned his instrument as carefully as any classical guitarist. The guitar he played after 1961 was a gift of the Newport Folk Foundation in appreciation of his appearance at the

Doc Reese, 1964

Elgia Hickok, 1964

Jimmie Tarlton, 1966

A. L. Lloyd, Willis James, Horton Barker,
and Sandy Paton, 1965

(Left) Bessie Jones and the Georgia Sea Island Singers, 1964

Skip James, 1964

Newport Folk Festival. To Mr. Hurt, the guitar was less an instrument than it was an equal partner in a two-member group.

Phrases of his songs passed from his mouth to the guitar strings and back again in an amiable dialogue. The strings alternated a set of bass and treble figures, moving often with a jogging ragtimey flavor, or becoming a gently philosophical extension of a voice used in similar fashion.

In a dark, lustrous, dulcetly projected voice that won attention rather than commanded it, Mr. Hurt sang sacred songs, blues or wry little erotic confections such as "Salty Dog" or "Candy Man." His repertory wasn't large, but it stood up beautifully on repeated hearings.

Always, John was the individualist. Despite his age and regional background, the traditional Mississippi Delta blues style of rough, tortured, intense singing and playing somehow never affected his approach. Rather, he was the meditative musical philosopher, with no forbidding regional dialect to make his lyrics difficult to follow.

Mississippi John Hurt was first recorded in 1928 by Okeh Records. Then he completely dropped from sight, playing only for occasional country dances and neighboring school and church functions.

In March, 1961, Tom Hoskins, a Washington disk collector, traced Mr. Hurt to his Mississippi home. Mr. Hoskins's only clue was a line from the old Okeh disk in which the singer referred to "Avalon" as his home town without any state mentioned. Mr. Hoskins told Mr. Hurt he was taking him to Washington to record him, but the singer was convinced that he "was an F.B.I. man." Said Hurt in 1962:

"I knew I hadn't done anything sinful, but I went along to Washington anyways. Now I'm sorry that F.B.I. man didn't come looking for me years ago."

So were many of us whose lives were enriched and extended by knowing John Hurt and his music. When he died in 1966, there

Bessie Jones, 1964

Clarence Ashley, 1963

(Below) Constance Seeger, Charles Seeger, Mike Seeger, and Roscoe Holcomb, 1965

(Below) Bessie Jones and the Georgia Sea Island Singers; Sacred Harp Singers *(Sitting)*, 1964

Bukka White, 1966

56

Moving Star Hall Singers, 1964

Robert Wilkensand and Skip James, 1964

Jim Garland, 1963

Big Joe Williams, 1966

Byron Berline, Kirk McGee, Eck Robertson, and Sam McGee, 1965

Son House, 1966

Rev. Gary Davis, 1964

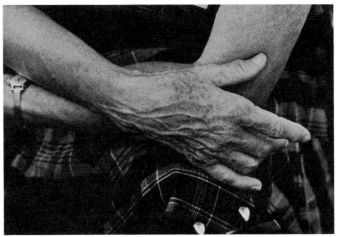

The hands of Almeda Riddle, 1964

The hands of Big Joe Williams, 1966

58

Joe Patterson, 1964

was a widespread feeling of personal loss to the folk-music community, for few country people had gotten closer to the city fan than John Hurt.

As symbol, as man and as musician, John Hurt typified the country person whose music formed a bridge to a more sophisticated culture. The folk fans stopped collecting records and songs and started collecting people. That was the moment of greatest humanity, greatest wholesomeness, and selflessness for the folk revival. It was perhaps the shining hour of American folk song.

Ollie Gilbert and Mrs. General Dixon Watson, 1964

Dock Boggs and Maria D'Amato, 1966

Merle Travis, 1967

Big Bill Broonzy, 1958

60

Doc Watson and son Merle Watson, 1964

Yank Rachel, Mississippi John Hurt, Skip James, Elizabeth Cotton, Doc Reese, Sleepy John Estes, 1964

Fred McDowell, 1964

Street guitarist, 1961

Arsenio Rodriguez, 1964

Frank Proffitt, 1964

Willie Dixon, Big Joe Williams, and
Memphis Slim, 1961

65

Elizabeth Cotton, 1964

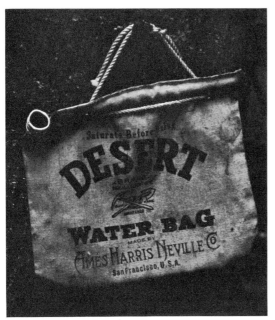

Billy Faier's water bag, 1964

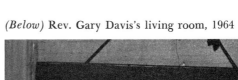

(Below) Rev. Gary Davis's living room, 1964

1962

1958

1963

Rev. Gary Davis's living room, 1964

71

III   EARLIER

FOLK REVIVALS

Because so much of what has happened in the history of folk song has been carried by word of mouth, we are forever trying to find out what happened before. Unlike the more well-established academic disciplines, folk music has not been clearly charted or historically documented. Mostly, we have to pull the story together from the old-timers who were there when it was happening.

As academic folklore becomes more of a fully accredited form of scholarship, the histories of earlier urban folk revivals will be published. For now, let us just throw out a few recollections, a few names, and a few episodes in the story of earlier folk revivals that antedate the last decade.

Scholars played a most important role in the past, for it was their inquiries, their books and monographs and their enthusiastic word-of-mouth that tried for so long to tell us about the great riches in our folk-song treasuries. Certainly one of the most important of these scholars was the nineteenth-century Harvard ballad scholar Francis James Child. Professor Child's landmark collection, *The English and Scottish Popular Ballads*, was a highlight of

74

1963

Dave Sear, Washington Square Park, 1958.

poetry and folklore scholarship of the nineteenth century. In league with other early folklore scholars, Child was primarily interested in the literary content of balladry, rather than in the musical or sociological aspects. He codified the 305 principal "classic" ballads of the English-speaking world in a canon that is still in use today to identify this or that ballad as variants of Child #12 or Child #205. Child's pioneering work has in recent years undergone the long-needed completion—with the addition of the music and its variants—by a zealous professor at the University of California at Berkeley, Bertrand Bronson. (The invaluable Bronson collection is being published by the Princeton University Press.)

Another giant in the study of folk song, John A. Lomax, was a different sort of researcher completely. Lomax did not work in the library, but took his research out into the field in the early 1900's. Beginning with his fascination with cowboy songs and the music of Texas Negroes, Lomax began a lifetime of ballad-hunting in search of musical Americana in the memories of the simple, common people of America. He and his son, Alan Lomax, who continued and expanded upon his father's work, were among the greatest collectors in the history of folk song. Long before the world, let alone the pop-music

1956

business, recognized the intrinsic worth in these simple tunes and ditties, the Lomaxes had tried to light the fires of enthusiasm among the leaders of the intellectual community toward folk song.

Still another famous pioneer collector was the Briton, Cecil Sharp, who carried his quest for old English songs to the Cumberland Mountains of Kentucky, where he was to find many English songs intact and in daily use by such singing families as the Ritchies of Viper, Kentucky.

Falling somewhere between the academics and the field collectors was the well-known writer Carl Sandburg. A poet in the grand tradition of Walt Whitman, Sandburg also

Girl in Washington Square Park

Ed Badeaux, 1966

Israel Young of Folklore Center, 1966

Moses Asch, 1958

Irwin Silber, 1966

Bruce Jackson, 1967

"heard America singing." He was also fascinated by the poetic outpouring he encountered in the farmhouses and ranch houses of America. While Sandburg was touring colleges in the late 1920's to do his research for his famous biography of Abraham Lincoln, he would support himself by singing folk tunes, and he ultimately issued one of the first and still most important collections of folk music, *The American Songbag*.

Charles Seeger, head of the famous folk-identified Seeger clan, was a musicologist at Harvard who early sensed the depth and substance of folk song. He went on to become one of the most highly regarded scientists who called themselves "ethno-musicologists." This new breed of scholar studied the musics of folk and primitive peoples stylistically, ethnologically, and comparatively with folk and refined musics of other cultures. The elder Seeger's zeal is reflected on a human level by all the children, from Pete to Mike to Peggy, who were to become the first family of American folk performers.

The early scholars who worked for pittances to enrich our knowledge of folk song are legion. It would include such men as Vance Randolph, Newman Ivey White, Dorothy Scar-

Jac Holzman, Theodore Bikel, Pete and Toshi Seeger, Harold Leventhal, Fred Hellerman, Maynard Solomon, 1965

80

Earl Robinson, 1963

borough, Samuel Bayard, and dozens of others. In our own period, just before the pop-folk movement exploded in 1957, there was a lot of serious work, collecting, publishing, and annotating being done by such scholars as Kenneth Goldstein, Richard Dorson, Mac-Edward Leach, John Greenway, Margaret Flanders, Archie Green, D. K. Wilgus, Fred Ramsey, Roger Abrahams, Ellen Stekert, Sam Charters, Harry Oster, and many, many more. (See Mr. Wilgus's account of all this in his excellent study, *Anglo-American Folksong Scholarship*.)

Although they were not scholars in the aca-

Paul Nelson, 1966

Alan Lomax, 1965

Marc Silber, 1966

81

Pete Seeger, 1959

Pete Seeger, 1962

Pete Seeger, 1958

demic sense, some of the best early work in folk-song was done for us by pioneer recording men. In the early 1920's, men such as Ralph Peer, Eli Oberstein, Frank Walker and Art Satherley were to record the first of blues and country performers. In one historic week in 1927, Ralph Peer made the first recordings of both the Original Carter Family and Jimmie Rodgers, two of the greatest names in the history of country music. It is a sad fact that only sporadic and incomplete accounts of the work of those early field recording giants have been left to us. In a later era, it was the devotional zeal of Moses Asch who was to capture

Pete Seeger, 1958

Pete Seeger and daughter Tinya, 1958

84

Pete Seeger, 1964

Constance Seeger, 1965

Pete Seeger and Paul Cadwell, 1964

Pete Seeger and family, 1958

Pete Seeger at Newport, 1966

Peggy Seeger, 1960

Pete Seeger, 1960

87

Pete Seeger, 1967

the best of America's and the world's folk music on such labels as Stinson, Asch, Disc, and finally Folkways. The story of Folkways alone would be a most exciting document of the great urban revival of the late 1930's and World War II era onward.

Inevitably, however, the story can be told in most romantic terms by the singers, rather than the scholars or recording officials. Because the folk movement is largely a romantic one, it is no surprise that it should revolve around certain figures who lives became so identified with song: such battlers for social justice as Aunt Molly Jackson, Jim Garland, The Dixon Brothers, and the folk man for all seasons, Joe Hill.

The urban East got wind of folk music through other performers, however, who were the first folk stars. The Kentuckian Burl Ives was to make the first major breakthrough to

Charles Seeger, 1965

Music and talking about music at Newport Folk Festival, 1965: Willis James, A. L. Lloyd, Charles Seeger, Alan Lomax, Samuel Bayard

Mike Seeger and two of his sons, 1965

The Seeger cabin

a mass audience for folk music with his lilting, unpressured way with a folk melody. Josh White of Greenville, South Carolina, was to fuse an intense sexuality with a highly personalized vocal and guitar style that was to make folk song the music of the city cabaret of the 1940's.

With the heavy interest in Negro life and culture that flowered during the era of President Franklin D. Roosevelt, Josh White also became spokesman and interpreter for Negro blues and religious song. At about the same time, the Chicago folk world took to its heart the late Big Bill Broonzy, a sophisticated

90

blues performer who, like Josh White, made the blues into both expression and entertainment for the white city audience.

The first major urban folk revival, during the 1940's, a period of national stress when both our democratic heritage and our celebration of minorities's contributions were similarly being heralded. As folk music became a viable entertainment medium for sophisticated audiences, a long and distinguished list of performing specialists emerged. Such a list included Richard Dyer-Bennet, John Jacob Niles, Cynthia Gooding, Oscar Brand, Joe and Tom Glazer, Marais and Miranda, John Langstaff, Sonny Terry and Brownie McGhee, Robin Roberts, Hermes Nye, Susan Reed, Paul Robeson, Earl Robinson, Harry and Jeannie West, and Hally Wood.

It is a sad commentary on time's erosion that many of these names are barely known today to the children of other folk fans now so aware of Joan Baez and Peter, Paul and Mary. A few of the older stalwarts continued to work right through the folk "arrival" of the 1940's into the "revival" of the 1960's, but in several cases, the audience cruelly discarded the pioneers, and scarcely reckoned with the strong contribution that they had made.

Two names that almost completely dominated the 1940's and have since become historical figures were those of Leadbelly and Woody Guthrie. Leadbelly, or Huddie Ledbetter, was a dynamic font of song. He was discovered by the Lomaxes in Louisiana State Prison at Angola in 1938 and sang his way to freedom. The enormous drive and energy of Leadbelly is hinted at by recordings on Folkways and Library of Congress, but his equal has still to be matched. Such symbolic songs as "Midnight Special" and "Goodnight, Irene" were trademarks of Leadbelly, still ringing down the years with his enormous vigor.

Although Woody Guthrie is still alive, illness has stilled his pen and his wonderfully craggy voice for more than a decade. Barely holding on to life is this great Oklahoma ballad-maker, poet, and performer, who per-

Kenneth Goldstein, 1966

Cynthia Gooding, 1960

91

Barbara Dane, 1965

Tony Kraber, 1967

Marion Distler of Folkways, 1959

1964

Sonny Terry, 1958

John Jacob Niles, 1959

Billy Faier, 1964

Bob Gibson, 1966

Lee Hayes, 1958

haps more than anyone, was to become the inspirational prototype of the wandering singer. Guthrie wrote more than a thousand songs, most of which were his own reworked versions of traditional songs, many learned from the repertory of The Carter Family. Guthrie was a true-to-life figure out of Steinbeck's *The Grapes of Wrath*, a little guy hemmed in by his environment and ultimately finding his own way of liberating himself from that environment.

You will all know such Guthrie songs as "So Long, It's Been Good to Know You," such children's masterpieces as "Car, Car," such evocations of a deep patriotism as "Pastures of Plenty," such a national folk anthem as "This Land Is Your Land." Guthrie was to fall in with early folk-community leaders like Will Geer, Millard Lampell, Alan Lomax, and Pete Seeger, and become intensely identified with the urban folk movement and radical politics. But Guthrie was too much of a genius

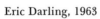
Eric Darling, 1963

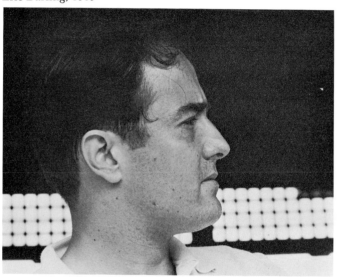

Fred Hellerman, 1958

Ronnie Gilbert, 1958

and an individualist to long remain totally identified with anything but his own art. His recordings and his writings should be studied by all who would understand what the American folk movement is about. Especially of interest are his early autobiography, *Bound for Glory*, and the recent Macmillan collection of his assorted writing called *Born to Win*.

The record of the early continuity in the importation of folk culture to the urban centers must next turn to Pete Seeger, The Al-

1960

The Weavers, 1960

97

Frank Warner, 1960

Clarence Cooper, 1967

manac Singers, The Weavers, and Harry Belafonte, each of whom were to be catalysts of enormous importance.

Pete Seeger would deny it, but he is clearly the father of the folk revival that began in 1958. A person of genuine modesty, Pete does not see any movement or broad-sweeping activity as the work of an individual, especially if he is the individual to be singled out. Let's say, then, that his talent, his zeal, his ability to turn a stonily silent audience into a joyful singing congregation—let's say that it is all these gifts of Pete Seeger that have turned the folk revival on.

Pete Seeger is one of those rare individuals in which the person, the philosophy, and the art are so well mixed that one is merely an extension of the other. He regards music as a quasi-religious spirit that can ennoble people and bring out their best. He regards folk

Brownie McGhee and daughter, 1959

Harry Smith, 1965

Ernie Marrs, 1959

Fiddler Bob Beers, 1965

Ed McCurdy and Eric Darling, 1959

Marilyn Child, 1960

Marshall Stearns, Barbara Dane, and Langston Hughes, 1959

Sam Eskin, 1964

Martha Schlamme and John Jacob Niles, 1959

Paul Clayton, 1959

Bess Hawes, 1963

Harry Smith, 1965

Cisco Houston, 1960

music as a brotherhood bridge on which communication and interraction and closeness can be built. All of this combines in the man who has been called "America's tuning fork" and "The Pied Piper of American folk music."

Again, Pete would modestly deny this and step to the rear of the stage, insisting that he only reflects the mood of the times, the attitudes of the audience, "the spirt of the age." Rather than dispute with a man who has tried over the years to heal so many family of folk music disputes, we can only say that Pete Seeger is largely responsible for keeping the spirit of the first city folk revival going during its difficult years in the early 1950's until it broke out again. Pete was also the guiding force behind such development as People's Songs and the establishment of *Sing Out!* magazine, and he was able to help get the Newport Folk Festival reorganized after it had been abandoned.

In the course of his long career in folk music, Pete was to be the pivotal figure with

101

Roscoe Holcomb and Jean Ritchie, 1965

Martha Schlamme and Frank Hamilton, 1959

Will Geer, 1960

(Below) Theodore Bikel, Oscar Brand, and Pete Seeger, 1967

Tom Paley, 1959

Oscar Brand, 1966

Hally Wood, 1965

Cisco Houston, 1960

two folk groups that were to be the precursors of the second revival—The Almanac Singers and The Weavers. The Almanacs were organized in the early 1940's by Pete, Millard Lampell, the writer, Woody Guthrie, and Butch Hawes. They named the group after their old residence, Almanac House, on 10th Street in Greenwich Village. Some of their recordings can still be heard, the first fascinating attempts to do folk music in group arrangements with a tangy, natural flavor.

The Weavers came together in 1948, the year of the famous third-party candidacy of Henry Wallace, and the last bountiful year for American radical political expression until

1960 signaled the end of McCarthyism. The Weavers—Seeger, Ronnie Gilbert, Lee Hays and Fred Hellerman—were born originally of the idea that the songs and drive of Leadbelly were so great it would take at least four other voices to do justice to them. After their first job at the Village Vanguard, The Weavers embarked on two years of folk popularity in which the national hit parade was ringing to the tunes of "Kisses Sweeter Than Wine" and "Goodnight, Irene."

Soon, however, the ominous work of the political blacklist was to gradually limit and finally force the disbandment of this pioneer pop-folk group. Harold Leventhal, who had been an important behind-the-scenes figure with The Weavers, was determined that The Weavers should rise, Phoenix-like, again, and he helped the group to reorganize again in 1956. This time they assembled for a historic reunion concert at Carnegie Hall and were to continue mainly as a recording group until 1964. In between time, each of The Weavers pursued individual careers, and Seeger was replaced, in succession, by Frank Hamilton, Erik Darling, and Bernie Krause.

Seeger continued his college concerts—building, always building an audience for work songs, lullabies, and spirituals, for international songs and banjo tunes. Although a few of the figures of the first revival and some other fine singers like Hally Wood and Ed McCurdy were thriving as performers, the two folk stars of the 1950's were Pete and Harry Belafonte.

Belafonte's approach was more stylized, personal, and polished than the folk world had known before. Although Belafonte's undeniably strong personality built a huge audience, he was often at a slight distance from the bulk of the folk movement. And yet, his role should not be slighted, as it has been by the folk "hippies" who found him overly "commercial." Belafonte had an unerring ear and sense of taste for the songs that meant so much to the folk audience. He was the focal point for a boom of another style of folk song, Calypso, in the mid-1950's, which was, in turn, to lead directly to the formation of The Kingston Trio and the exciting musical decade that followed.

Woody Guthrie's fiddle, 1959

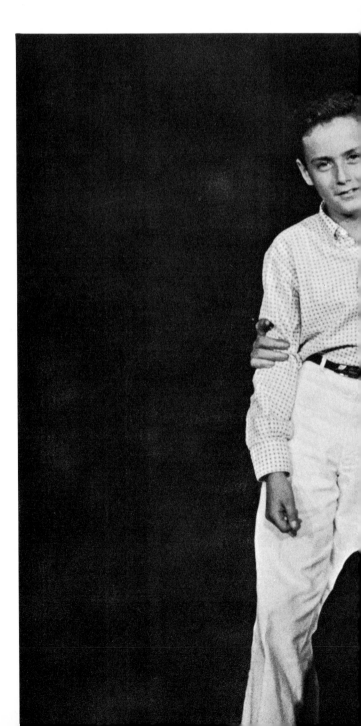

Will Holt, 1960.

Sam Hinton, 1963

Woody Guthrie and family, 1960

Izzy Young, 1967

IV   THE BIG REVIVAL

1958 TO TOMORROW

It was a gathering storm, a storm-driven fad, a social movement, a mania, a cultural epidemic. The big folk boom which started in 1958 and is still with us can be called all these things, whether one takes a positive or negative view of the breadth and depth of the folk craze.

Some of us would have wished that it had emerged with a little less frenzy, a little less hoopla and compulsiveness, but these seem to be as much a part of the fabric of American life as the strong threads of tradition that hold the substance together.

For all the reasons that we have already discussed, the climate was building toward a major change in American popular musical taste. The rock 'n' roll movement had been running its course for three years and seemed to have hit a stone wall in creativity. Calypso had had its brief hour on the stage—pleasing, infectious, novel, and clever. It forecast another time of mass song-writing, of instant poetry, of musical versifying that was to be as close to our idiom as Calypso was to the Trinidadians.

Moving logically out of the interest in Calypso and all things Caribbean came a group from the West Coast called The Kingston Trio—Nick Reynolds, Dave Guard and Bob Shane—who had a decided American-cum-Caribbean flavor. They used conga drums and were playfully full of energy, tumbling

around the stage with youthful drive. And yet The Kingston Trio was as home-made as applie pie; most of their songs had nothing whatsoever to do with Calypso. One song, for instance, "Tom Dooley," was a Southern mountain ballad that Frank Warner had collected from the late Frank Proffitt. That song was clearly emblematic of the beginning of the major folk-revival of the last decade.

The Kingston Trio probably felt it was simply a pop group working in a new idiom, but the threesome achieved more than it ever dreamed. It lighted a fire in the juke-box, on the radio station, in the music and record shop, on the college campus, in the emerging national coffeehouse movement.

Not everyone, of course, was pleased with the style of the Kingston Trio. Nothing so indicated the strong lines of contrast and dissent as two performances at the very first Newport Folk Festival, in July, 1959. The Kingston Trio was the extroverted box-office attraction, billed as the leading attraction for the total of 13,000 paid admissions for the festival. But to underline the difference, a few hundred persons, at least, were just as keen to listen to the delicate, introverted traditional songs of Jean Ritchie, the girl who, to use Ed McCurdy's phrase, "had left the mountains although the mountains had never left her." For many in the Newport audience, the folk melodies and dulcimer of Jean Ritchie were

a language apart, a bit hard to understand, a bit tame for tastes honed only on the exuberant dynamism of The Kingston Trio.

These were the two polarities of the early phases of this folk boom—show business and traditional song. But as the years went on, both show business and traditional music and musicians prospered. Each taught the other and each finally ended up being influenced by the other. Soon traditional performers were becoming "ethnic stars" and pop stars were rearranging ethnic song. It was a curious and often confounding interrelationship.

Those days of the late 1950's seemed, to any chronicler or student, like an explosion. Everyone, it seemed, or nearly everyone, was

112

turning from hobbyist musician into a professional. Groups sprang up like crabgrass: The Limeliters, The Brothers Four, The Chad Mitchell Trio, Peter, Paul and Mary. There were similarities and stylistic relationships, but there was also the quest for group identity and individuality. The Weavers, which had stood as an inspiration for many later folk groups, continued, but finally disbanded at the end of 1963 at a sentimental farewell concert in Chicago's Orchestra Hall.

But the pioneering of The Weavers, if not forgotten, was to dim in memory as such groups as those mentioned above and The

Tarriers, The Rooftop Singers and The Highwaymen and dozens of others sprouted up to follow more directly in the pattern of The Kingston Trio.

Similarly, there was a rather sad "changing of the guard" as individual new luminaries gradually eclipsed some of the important older stars. Odetta, whose huge and majestic alto seemed to rock the very earth, took over where Cynthia Gooding had held quiet sway. Bob Gibson came, all too briefly, to the fore. Billy Faier and Dave Van Ronk and Jack Elliott were among the first second-level performers to develop their followings. Able, earnest

113

Buffy Sainte-Marie, 1963

Buffy Sainte-Marie, 196[

Hedy West, 1967

Carolyn Hester, 1965

The Von Schmidt Family, 1965

115

Tom Paxton, 1964

Richie Havens, 1965

Bill McAdoo, 1960

Artie Traum, 1966

John Herald, 1963

The Greenbriar Boys, 1964

craftsmen like Richard Dyer-Bennet were pushed temporarily to the wayside. It was a game of constantly shifting musical chairs in which performers had their brief, brief hour of fame, or built a steadily growing following.

In the cities, the folk revival found almost any setting around which to cluster. The open-air sings in Manhattan's Washington Square Park were one of the more colorful nuclei. There, on Sunday afternoons throughout the fifties and sixties (except for a sad period in the spring of 1961 when an ill-

advised Parks Commissioner turned off the sound of people) was a lively forum for folk singers. Roger Sprung and Erik Weissberg, two youngsters who had been fascinated with the technical potential of the five-string banjo, were as much products of the Sunday music sessions in the Greenwich Village square as they were of any school. Flocking around the open fountain were hundreds of young music-lovers and visitors, mostly, it seems, attracted to the sounds of city Bluegrass music.

Coincident with the folk revival was the

117

The Rooftop Singers, 1963

(Below) Leon Bibb, 1959

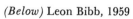

Sandy and Jeanie, 1966

118

Eric Andersen and Debby Green, 1966

Mike Settle, 1963

Kim Loy Wong, University Settlement Steel Band, 1960

Long John Miles, 1966

Logan English, 1960

119

Joan Baez, 1964

Joan Baez, 1965

Joan Baez, 1965

Joan Baez and Donovan, 1965

120

Joan Baez, 1965

Joan Baez, 1965

Joan Baez holding Bob Dylan, 1964

Joan Baez, 1965

Joan Baez, 1967

121

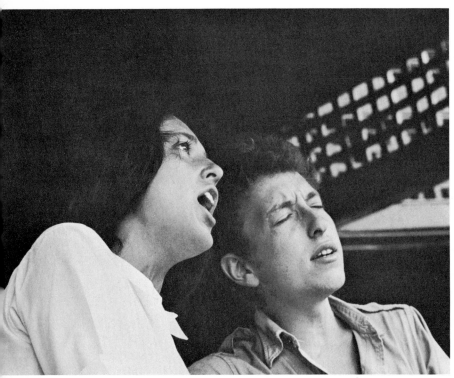

Joan Baez and Bob Dylan, 1963

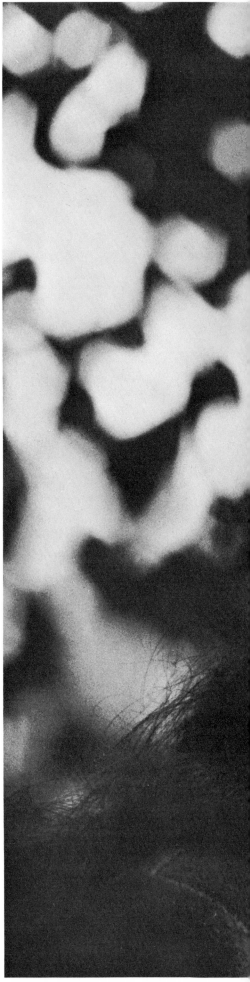

Joan Baez, 1964

122

Bob Dylan and Bill Lee, 1963

Bob Dylan, 1963

Bob Dylan, 1963

Bob Dylan, 1963

Bob Dylan, 1964

Bob Dylan, 1962

Bob Dylan, 1963

Bob Dylan, 1964

Bob Dylan, 1963

125

Mitch Greenhill, 1964

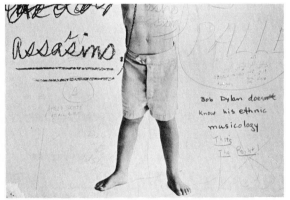

1963

Bob Jones, 1964

Bernie Kraus, 1964

Marilyn Kweskin and daughter, 1966

Julius Lester and daughter, 1965

José Feliciano, 1965

Theodore Bikel, 1964

national boom of the coffeehouse. Here was the perfect solution, it seemed, for "a community living room." As the members of the silent generation came out from behind the McCarthy era blanket of conformity and fear, they were looking for a place to socialize, to listen to the new-wave irreverent comics, and to hear and sing along with the new folk celebrities. From The Gaslight and Bitter End in New York to the Ten O'Clock Scholar in Minneapolis, Philadelphia's Second Fret, Cambridge's Club 47, to coffeehouses like The Inquisition in Vancouver and The Ice House in Pasadena, a new generation found a new place to hang-out.

Some of the more formal nightclubs and brand-new cabarets took the folk boom a step further. The Village Gate, The Purple Onion, the hungry i, Gerdes' Folk City, The Gate of Horn, and dozens of lesser-known cabarets began to feature folk singers and instrumentalists. It seemed as though someone had tapped a well and the gushers of talent sprang out in never-ending profusion. The audience listened to Casey Anderson, Hoyt Axton, Fiddler Beers, Leon Bibb, Theo Bikel, Sandy Bull, Judy Collins, Bonnie Dobson, Logan English, Carolyn Hester, Ian and Sylvia, Jim and Jean, Phil Ochs, Lisa Kindred, and on and on through the alphabet and the night.

128

Judy Collins, 1964

dy Collins and Theodore Bikel, 1963

Judy Collins, 1965

Judy Collins, 1967

129

Paul Stookey, 1965

A few national festivals and many local festivals began to take the measure of all this activity. Attendance at the Newport Festival grew and grew. After the interruption caused by a riot outside a jazz festival in 1960, the Newport Folk Festival was reconstituted by George Wein, Pete Seeger, and Theo Bikel on a non-profit basis, being run by a rotating board of musicians.

Some of the greatest moments in all our memories of the revival will be attached to the festivals at Newport. Newport reflected the hootenanny craze of 1963 and the strong surge of the civil rights movement, marked the ever-growing interest in native ethnic performers, and the difficult balance between star and obscure talent which followed. By 1964

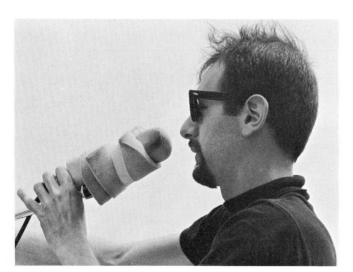

Peter Yarrow, 1965

Peter, Paul and Mary, 1964

Peter, Paul and Mary, 1965

Peter, Paul and Mary, 1965

Newport's Folk Festival had eclipsed its parent jazz festival in power, audience, and number of participating performers.

But Newport, as an important national focal point, was only one of many excellent and representative festivals., Yale undergraduates had a series of fine festivals at Indian Neck, near Branford, Connecticut; the students at the Universities of California and Chicago mounted the most ambitious festivals at three campuses, replete with stimulating workshops and seminars and some memorable programs. Long before, the pioneering students at tiny Swarthmore College in Pennsylvania had begun its series of folk festivals in the late 1940's but naturally the tempo quickened in the late 1950's and early 1960's. (Swarthmore, in 1966, was again to blaze a trail, turning much of its folk-festival energies toward folk rock and hard rock in what was probably the first student-run rock 'n' roll festival.)

In the fall of 1962, the American Broadcasting Company TV network began a program that was to give still another shot in the arm to the folk revival as well as to cause a decided controversy about which way the revival was to go. The show, called "Hootenanny," was named after that curious Americanism for sing-alongs that Pete Seeger and Woody Guthrie had earlier popularized. As the mechanics of show business took over, there was to be almost a surfeit of folk recordings and performers. There were to be even "Hootenanny" boots for sale. For a time, two get-rich-quick-or-perish magazines, carrying the Hootenanny emblem, were produced by the ever-present American publisher looking to cash in on a craze.

All of this the old-guard folk fans viewed with alarm and felt that their thunder had been stolen and distorted. To a degree they were right, for the greatest irony of the "Hootenanny" show was that the patriarch of the revival, Pete Seeger, was not allowed to appear. Pete's old left-wing orientation was to be a recurring source of repression and blacklisting against him, despite the fact that he was

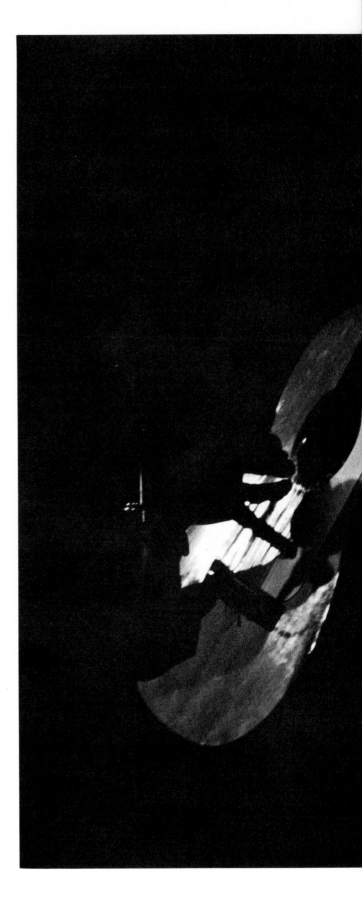

Mary Travers, 1964

Peter LaFarge, 1962

Alex Lukeman, 1963

fully exonerated of contempt of Congress upon court appeal.

A boycott against the show was started by a group of singers, led initially by Judy Collins and Carolyn Hester, and was to generally tear the folk community in half. Some performers felt the show would become even worse esthetically if the boycott robbed it of the people who knew what folk music was all about. Some adamantly refused to appear, feeling that "no Pete Seeger, no me." (In many ironic instances performers who had never been asked on the TV show waved highest the banner of opposition, and in other cases pop groups who had nothing to gain commercially from the show refused to appear for business-office reasons, but let the impression spread that they were avoiding the show for the highest of ideals.)

What final estimation can we make of the

134

(*Opposite page*) Jack Elliott, 1964

Mimi Fariña and a young Von Schmidt, 1965

Beth Van Over, 1965

Yomo Toro Group, 1966

hootenanny fad division of the folk-music revival? Pro and con must be the answer. The TV show itself was among the weakest esthetic adventures in the history of either the TV medium or the music world. There was also a basic disbelief and lack of understanding in folk song reflected in the show that had nothing to do with preferences for pop-folk over traditional folk. Partially because of the blacklist against Seeger, many of the best interpreters were denied to the show and this, in turn, may have ultimately been self-defeating after the initial strong protest was made.

As to the larger fad, it did almost become a study in excesses, where clapping along to shaky and nonprofessional performers became the order of the day. The integrity of folk song was assailed by the fad, but it was not an altogether negative phenomenon. There were quality performers, such as Doc Watson and Maybelle Carter, on the TV show who would otherwise have never enjoyed so vast an audience. A lot of quality seeped through the porous rocks, and there were provocative and interesting articles and issues of the two *Hootenanny* magazines (one edited by Linda Solomon, the other by this writer.) The debate could go on forever and perhaps never reach a conclusion.

Some of the élitist snobs of folk song were intrinsically unhappy that their private little enclave had become common property. Some of them, of vaguely socialist leanings, were hard-put to explain the contradiction in their philosophy and their subjective feelings at this distribution of even a watered-down folk soup. Probably the best estimation of the two-year "hootenanny" craze is that it did as much good in broadening the appreciation of folk song as it did harm. We survived it. Folk music survived it. Publishing and TV survived, and so we relegate it to the history of curious American phenomena.

As the folk revival moved on from the shambles of its hootenanny phase, a newer, often more sophisticated critic stepped forward. Using the standards of other musics, with a disdain for the essentially youthful nature of the revival and its obvious liberal-

Judy Roderick, 1966

The Pennywhistlers, 1966

Bonnie Dobson, 1964

137

radical orientation, such critics as Jean Shepherd and Gene Lees took to their typewriters to denigrate topical song, folk song, and to heap generous portions of ridicule upon the whole revival. A few of us wasted some time and energy on rebutting Shepherd and Lees, when we should have realized that they were really calling more attention to themselves by being gadflies rather than serious critics.

A more knowledgeable critic of the folk boom, Bob Reisner, a jazz lover, took exception to the folk boom in *The Village Voice* in early 1960. I replied to him, in part:

"There is no more menace of folk music's 'driving classical and jazz albums out of homes' than there is a menace that do-it-yourself carpentry will put an end to Chippendale or Swedish Modern. For a host of wholesome reasons, people are rediscovering and communicating pleasure in making music for themselves . . .

"Folk music will not cure dandruff, schizophrenia, or the problem of the hydrogen

Chris Smither, 1967

139

Sandy Paton, 1966

Phil Ochs, 1963

Caroline Paton, 1966

The Tarriers, 1960

Guy Carawan and son

Mark and Kathy Spoelstra, 1965

140

Harry Belafonte, 1965

bomb. It is no panacea for the malaise of modern man. But the revival that alarms and confounds Reisner is demonstrably one of the healthiest and most democratizing cultural phenomena going on in America today. The flood of world folk-music recordings issued in the last few years, which Reisner might explore along with his 'Mozart and Miles', constitute nothing less than a musical and ethnographic Baedeker of man.

"The sensitive listener can, through his home phonograph, travel to the highlands of Bolivia, the farms of Bulgaria, the thickets of Africa, or the ranges of Australia. He can, with careful listening, familiarize himself with the ethos of the peoples who live there.

"It is for solid esthetic reasons that folk song fascinated and influenced Vaughan Williams, Kodaly, Copland, Bartók, Schubert, Mahler, and Shostakovich. It is also increasingly attracting the attention of many jazz men such as Fred Katz, Dave Brubeck, John Benson Brooks, Herbie Mann, and Art Blakey. But why must Reisner pit one form against the other? The standards that govern classical and jazz composition and performance are totally different than those governing folk music. To listen and judge one by the criteria of the other is fallacious and unjust . . ."

So ended another one of the wrangles that seemed to add sport and zest to the folk scene.

141

Izzy's Back Room at old Folklore Center

Many outside our folk world seem to think that folk fans do nothing but dispute, and it is really quite amazing to find how much discord exists in a field with such a basically idealistic background as the folk world. The reasons are easy to advance.

Several of the early figures in folk song were tirelessly battling for acceptance. They almost felt a need to shout their enthusiasms, their demand for recognition for a cultural form that was so often vilified and downgraded. A champion of this underdog art form, like Alan Lomax, got so accustomed to fighting that it became a life-style, and he continued to fight long after the need to battle snobbism had vanished. Similarly, another pioneer, Moses Asch, had gone bankrupt several times and endured a great deal of personal privation

1967

144

Jerry Silverman and The Harvesters, 1962

and loss before his identification with folk music paid off.

For other folk wranglers, there was simply a mistaken identification of their total social-revolutionary interests with folk song. Thus we have a column by the businessman-cum-rebellion leader, Irwin Silber, called "Fan the Flames," in the leading folk-song magazine, *Sing Out!* The obvious anomalous confusion of roles is apparent to almost all but the flame-fanner.

Still another battler type comes from the purist sect, which measures everything by standards so sacrosanct that he must isolate change from the continuum of life. Britain probably has more folk-purists than we do, and also has a greater proportion of those who would toss out shifting standards as a sign of weakness. One of the more urbane British commentators on folk song, A. L. Lloyd, is willing to admit that the early years of the revival saw so many shaky standards and attitudes that it was a matter of "the blind leading the blind." This has largely kept the development of a mature folk-song criticism and commentary at a rudimentary stage. As a practitioner fighting an often lonely attempt to set up flexible, workable standards, I can safely say that folk journalism is thirty years behind jazz journalism.

The final, most omnipresent type of folk battler is one that must perforce be described as "the loser." He is the person so embroiled with personal, often financial, frustrations and such an over-all hostile attitude toward any organized activity that he must pick fights and battles. The loser resents the money that professionals make on folk song, resents the star system, and resents the fact that a major social-musical movement may have crested and passed without his voice becoming a dominant one or a highly remunerated one. This is a type as familiar from coast to coast in the folk movement as is the angry, frustrated jazz-man who has been denied his own outlet, frequently by his own limitations as much as by a competitive atmosphere.

To such discouraging precepts as these

146

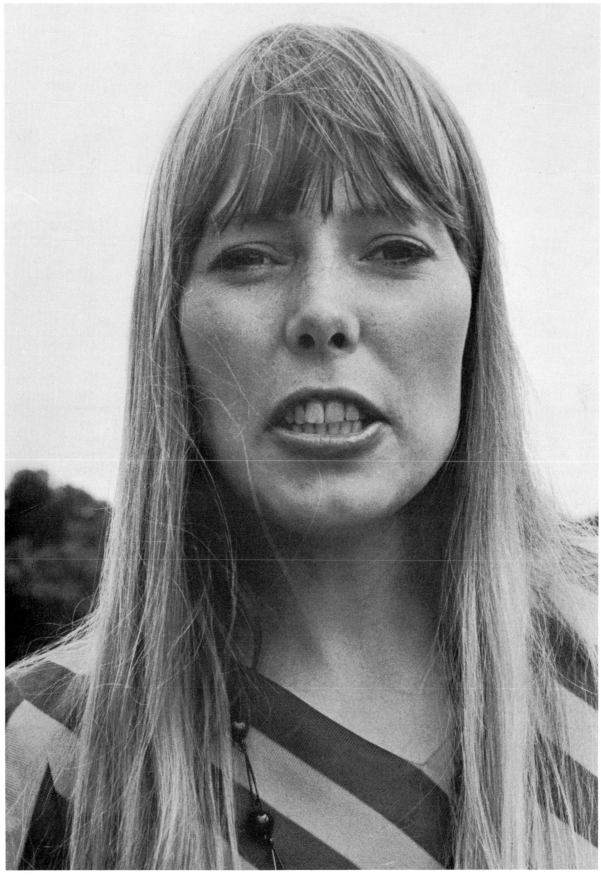

Joni Mitchell, 1967

Rory Biehusen and Thiele, 1968

Marie D'Amato with newborn, 1965

Odetta, 1959

comes the relieving and warming presence of those to whom Pete Seeger has been more than a musical leader. Seeger, not without his own strong sensibilities and reactions however, has set a model for acceptance, flexibility and the ability to listen to currents and changes. Rather than be negative, he will always stress the positive aspects of a new development, accentuate the affirmative. Were there more people making good musical and maturely logical sense as Pete Seeger, the whole folk movement would have made greater progress a lot earlier than it did.

But most of the reasons for the seemingly endless disputes of folk song seem to lie in two factors: (1) It is essentially a youth movement, and young people are battling their way toward their own standards and rules and fighting the inexplicable things of the past. (2) Idealistically impelled movements are constantly running into contradictions in a society that has all but forgotten its idealism. The impact of commercialism and the attendant need and desire to make money have caused problems every step of the folk road. Had the leadership been a little more helpful

Kathy and Carol, 1965

John Hammond, 1963

Donovan and some of his audience, 1965

Donovan, 1965

155

Arlo Guthrie, Clarence Cooper, and Peter Bellamy, 1967

Happy Traum, 1968

John Fahey, 1968

Hamilton Camp, 1965

158

159

Bruce Murdock, 1965

Jim and Jean, 1965

Eric Weissberg,
John Cohen, and Tom Paley,
1959

160

in offering guidance on this score, perhaps there would have been less professional jealousy, less carping, less competition and maneuvering for coveted places.

But let us not let this frank discussion of the problems of the folk revival outweigh its over-all value. The dissemination of knowledge and recorded or live performances of folk and folk-derived musical expression has been one of the marvels of our time. It has opened countless doors on experience and understanding of those who have been the overlooked little people of our world. That has been an enormous achievement, and that is why the folk-music revival is a perpetual one. Folk music is here to stay.

Jackie Washington, 1963

162

Emmy Lou Harris

Ralph Rinzler, 1965

Tom Rush, 1965

Carolyn Hester, 1966

165

167

V   A SONG OF

PRAISE AND A SONG OF FREEDOM

Negro music became "functional"—the textbook definition of some sorts of folk music—when it went to church. It also went modern, throwing those who use textbook definitions of such a dynamic as folk song quite off their pat position.

The glory and the sanctity of the traditional Negro spiritual has undergone so much change in contemporary life that city folk fans had to search to find the spiritual in its "pure" form. For anyone interested in rapid movement, change, flux, and adaptation of tradition, the music of the Negro in its modern gospel applications and its subsequent use in the civil rights movement is one of the most exciting stories of the entire folk revival. This chapter will limn the emergence of modern gospel and of the freedom song, two variations on the theme of praise and salvation.

Negro gospel music has spread far from the churches in which it was born. During the late 1950's and 1960's, the fervor and vibrancy

170

Dorothy Love and the Gospel Harmonettes, Swan Silvertones, and Dixie Hummingbirds, 1966

Moving Star Hall Singers, 1964

of Negro religious music had invaded the theater, the music festival, and even, for a brief time, the night club.

Musical elements of gospel have spawned a new school of jazz performance, played a role as "freedom songs" in the integration movement, made a deep impress on popular music, and become a solidly entrenched subdivision of American folk music.

This impact of a religious music on popular art and entertainment may well be without precedent in the history of the church, although the development of the folk mass, the jazz mass, and even the rock 'n' roll mass of the mid-1960's was clearly following a pattern long since established by Negro gospel song.

It was partially out of a need to make the music of the church vital to the congregants that modern gospel music developed. It began to take its present form after World War I, but its roots can be traced much farther back than that.

What is gospel music? It may be composed of traditional music of varying moods and tempos, using either biblical or colloquial language. Its lyrics may be simple in sentiment, but are always sacred, inspirational, and devotional in content.

Perhaps the most exciting and curious aspect of gospel song is that these sacred, devotional words are generally wedded to music and instruments that are so secular as to be indistinguishable from jazz, blues, or even rock 'n' roll. Modern gospel is a strongly improvisational music, in which the voices of gospel singers play freely as if they were instruments in a jazz ensemble. In many churches of the "Sanctified" and "Holiness" sects jazz instruments are used along with voices.

What seems most overwhelming to new listeners of gospel song is the total abandon and fervor of the performances. Wellsprings of energy seem to open up, as the singers get themselves more deeply involved in the surging rhythms, exultant crescendos, and the enveloping descants.

There was a time, not long ago, when many Negro church leaders looked with disfavor on the secular nature of gospel music. Many churches with large Negro congregations continue to use the standard formal music of the hymnal. But the majority of Negro congregations have made the transition to the new blues-based, gospel song. It has been estimated that there are some five hundred amateur gospel groups in the country and more than fifty professional groups.

Some of the professional gospel singers are widely known. Mahalia Jackson, daughter of

Rev. and Mrs. Pearly Brown, 1966

a New Orleans pastor, is undoubtedly the reigning queen. Her rich, full contralto has proselytized earnestly for gospel around the world. Marion Williams and the Stars of Faith, working in the gospel show "Black Nativity," with a script by the distinguished writer Langston Hughes, brought one form of gospel to millions who may never have heard it within the precincts of a church.

Many other names of distinctive gospel stylists spring to mind: The Staple Singers, a family quartet from Mississippi by way of Chicago. Interestingly enough, the Staples won the *Down Beat* award for the best vocal group of 1962. Other names, other styles: James Cleveland, The Caravans, The Clara Ward Singers, The Soul-Stirrers, The Highway Q.C.'s, Ernestine Washington, The Five Blind Boys, The Stevens Singers, The Abyssinian Baptist Chorus, The Drinkard Singers, Maceo Woods, Carrie Smith, The Roberta Martin Singers, Alex Bradford, The Gospel Pearls, The Swan Silvertones, Tabernacle Singers,

The Grandison Singers . . . a long and distinguished list, by no means complete.

Although there was a cresting of interest in gospel in 1962–1963, when many major record companies were signing up gospel performers, the majority record on somewhat minor or specialized labels, such as Savoy, Tabernacle, Battle, Peacock, etc.

Many pop-music listeners were drawn to gospel indirectly. When they realized that a lot of the "soul" and easy fluidity of the singing of Ray Charles was called "churchy" among the initiate, they tried to track the music back to its origins. Similar graduates of gospel singing are Della Reese, Aretha Franklin, Sammy Price and Dionne Warwick.

Around 1955, the jazz world began to feel and absorb the impact of gospel energy. The "soul jazz" movement borrowed heavily from the cadences, tempos, and spirit, if not the letter, of congregation singing. Among those whose jazz improvisations began to reflect church sounds were Cannonball Adderly,

The Clara Ward Singers, 1960

Dr. Willis James, 1966

Bobby Timmons, Horace Silver, and the fine organist, Jimmy Smith.

Because gospel music, like its parent churches, is a missionary vehicle, there has always been an attempt to persuade and win converts. Few developments in this out-of-church work held more interest than its sorties into American night life. In the late 1940's a few singers tried gospel music in the cabarets, but often at the expense of outraging the devout.

Sister Rosetta Tharpe, Brother John Sellers,

Alex Bradford and his Gospel Group, 1959

174

Rev. Robert Wilkens, 1964

Mavis Staples, 1964

Richie Havens, 1968

175

and The Grandison Singers were the bold pioneers of this cabaret gospel, and they were often ostracized in the Negro community for doing it. At one point Clara Ward had one group bearing her name working in Birdland, the jazz club, while another was in Las Vegas. But the move into the cabarets went too far for the religionists with the launching of a pop-gospel movement and the opening of The Sweet Chariot, a rather tawdry midtown Manhattan club built around gospel song. Leaders of gospel, from Mahalia Jackson down, saw the apparent distortion of the basic devotional content of the music, and soon the band-

wagon gospel-cabaret fad went the way of all fads.

Despite these forays, gospel continues to flourish in its native environments from impoverished storefront congregations to more affluent tabernacles. Radio evangelists such as the Elder Solomon Lightfoot Michaux, Elder Beck and the Rev. C. L. Franklin have done much to spread gospel music into many homes since the heyday of radio in the 1930's. There is scarcely a major urban center that does not have its Sunday gospel programs on radio today.

The history of gospel song is as complex

176

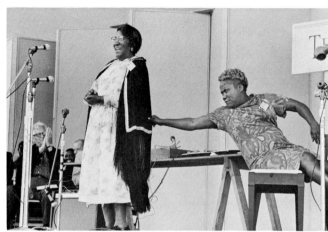

(*Left, pictures one through three*)
Katy Bell Nubin and
Sister Rosetta Tharpe, 1967

Some of the Georgia Sea Island Singers, 1964

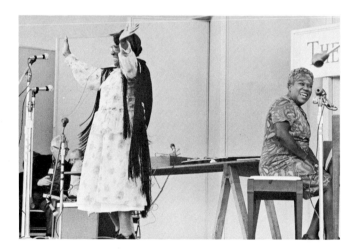

(*Below*) Chambers Brothers, 1965

The Dixie Hummingbirds, 1966

Odetta, 1964

and interfoliated as that of Negro religious music itself. Several kindred traditions have been tributaries to the mainstream of gospel music: the traditions of the spiritual, the jubilee, the hymn, and the anthem. C. Albert Tindley, who is regarded by some as the father of modern gospel, was writing religious songs around the turn of the century, drawing upon the styles of spirituals and other traditional religious forms.

In the 1920's, Thomas A. (Georgia Tom) Dorsey, an itinerant blues piano-player, began to fuse the music of the blues with the message of the church. Mr. Dorsey and Lucie Campbell are among the leading composers of gospel songs.

But gospel is less a question of the music than it is of the performing style, wherein lies the magic. Langston Hughes has written:

"Negro gospel singing is folk singing, in that in the pure state it never follows arrangements or pat notations. Should this happen, it is a sign that they have ceased to be gospel singers and have become mere entertainers."

Some of the best milieus for hearing gospel music remain deep in the Negro community, in church, or such theaters as Manhattan's Apollo, where the amount of involvement and rapport between the "preaching" singers is so great that women in the congregation are known to faint with transcendence. Still another place to hear the surfacing of gospel song and with salvation linked to earthly and immediate needs is in the civil rights movement.

Although the "freedom-song movement" was to burst with full fervor during the heart of the civil rights sit-in action that began in

178

True Vine Singers, 1967

Dorothy Love and the Gospel Harmonettes, 1966

Staple Singers, 1967

1960, there was ample existence of a long, involved tradition of Nego "protest" song.

But it was during the peak of the civil rights movement that Negro folk music, which had been singing of a promised land since the days of slavery, became a vital force in the attempts to fulfill that promise in the South.

In the course of a survey for *The New York Times* in August, 1962, I was to find that integration leaders were all in agreement that music set the tempo of their movement. During visits to Albany, Georgia; Durham, North Carolina; and other tension points throughout the South, I was to find ample evidence that spirituals, hymns, and gospel songs were helping to bolster the morale of integrationists and to disarm the segregationists of their hostility.

In the early 1960's a new tributary of "freedom songs," bold words set to old melodies, was making the deep river of Negro protest in song run swifter. The songs, old and new, were used at mass meetings, demonstrations, prayer vigils on Freedom Rides, in jails, and before sit-ins.

The music rang with the bombast of election songs, the sanctity of marching tunes for a holy crusade and the spirit-building of fraternity anthems.

"The freedom songs are playing a strong and vital role in our struggle," the Rev. Dr. Martin Luther King Jr., president of the Southern Christian Leadership Conference, told me in Albany, Georgia. "These songs give the people new courage and a sense of unity. I think they keep alive a faith, a radiant hope in the future, particularly in our most trying hours," Dr. King went on.

The Albany Movement was a coalition of civil rights groups that struggled through 1962 to break down racial segregation in the southwest Georgia city. More than 1,100 arrests were made there in that period. A young Negro leader in Albany, Charles Jones, said emphatically: "There could have been no Albany movement without music. The field secretary for the Student Non-violent Coordinating Committee went on: "We could not have communicated with the masses of the people

179

Aretha Franklin, 1968

Aretha Franklin, 1968

180

Aretha Franklin, 1968

Aretha Franklin, 1968

Aretha Franklin, 1968

Aretha Franklin, 1968

Aretha Franklin and Musicians, 1968

without music. They could not have communicated with us without music. They are not articulate. But through songs, they expressed years of suppressed hope, suffering, even joy and love."

In Albany, one could hear the majestic old spiritual:

Go down, Moses,
'Way down in Egypt's land,
Tell old Pharaoh,
To let my people go.

But, minutes later, one could hear a young Negro, who talked of "the new-time religion," singing to the same melody:

Go down, Kennedy,
'Way down in Georgia land.
Tell old Pritchett
To let my people go.

(Old Pritchett is Chief of Police Laurie Pritchett of Albany.)

Sacred Harp Singers, 1964

Sacred Harp Singers, 1964

Watson Family, 1964

The Stanley Brothers, 1964

This song illustrates the "freedom song" activity, the changing of lyrics to suit the immediate situation, which swept the South by word of mouth, through mimeographed song-sheets, and through other quick methods of improvised dissemination.

Freedom songs of the early 1960's and their counterpart in the Northern topical-protest song movement represent perhaps the greatest mass topical song-writing sweep to have affected America since the days of the organizing drives of the labor movement in the 1930's. The songs were to be fully as controversial as those of the earlier labor movements, including the era of Wobbly songs.

But it was not only the new and more militant lyrics that were taking a strong catalytic role in the civil rights struggle. A Georgia official of the National Association for the Advancement of Colored People recalled the power of traditional religious music at an organizing meeting of the Hart County Chapter in Hartwell. Remarked Vernon E. Jordan, Jr.:

"The people were cold with fear. Music did

Dorothy Love, 1966

Cape Breton Singers, 1965

183

Moving Star Hall Singers, 1964

what prayer and speeches could not do in breaking the ice."

Although there have been many recordings of freedom songs, and they have been transplanted to concert and festival stages, these "performances" pale beside the real thing—watching and hearing the music being used in a "functional" situation. Gloster B. Current, national director of branches of the N.A.A.C.P., summed this up:

"They cannot hold a mass meeting in the South without music. You should really go there and hear it on the spot. The music sounds much different under the gun."

Recordings and Northern concerts have long tended to make freedom songs sound like rather stale tub-thumping and sloganeering. Instead, you must visualize, if you can, a group of forty to fifty young Negroes on the stairs of a Southern church after a mass meeting. History put these "average" Negro teen-agers in front of a microphone, and they are aware that the whole world is listening. A young woman on the steps of an Albany church chants:

Over my head I see freedom in the air,
There must be a God somewhere.

As Bernice Johnson sings, one can see, over her shoulder, a prowl car passing three times within fifteen minutes.

For an inkling of the emotional impact of freedom songs in action, imagine a crowded, sweaty meeting in Albany's Mount Zion Bap-

184

tist Church. The heat broils mercilessly, despite six electric fans and dozens of hand-held paper fans. Dr. King and his aide, the Rev. Ralph D. Abernathy, have spoken to their followers. The meeting closes with the traditional singing of "We Shall Overcome," which has been called "the 'Marseillaise' of the Negro rights revolution."

(The story of "We Shall Overcome" is a fascinating case of a transplanted folk song that was probably born in the formal hymnal, as "I'll Overcome, Someday." It was taken over by certain Food and Agricultural or Negro Textile Union workers in the 1940's, transported to the Highlander Folk School, then in Mounteagle, Tennessee. The late Zilphia Horton made it into the school's theme song, from which Guy Carawan, a central figure in the freedom-song movement was to pass it to the sit-in movement. The majestic soaring breadth of the song is sung with hands clasped with neighbors as rows of singers sway in rhythm to the music.)

Tired, dejected, almost pessimistic rights activists have found as much solace and strength in the music of the integration movement as have worshippers through gospel song. They are variations on a theme, and are rooted deeply in Negro tradition.

Guy Carawan was to play a catalytic role in spreading the freedom song throughout the South much as Pete Seeger was to be the Johnny Appleseed of folk song in the North. Carawan did not invent this use of protest song, for it goes back to pre-Civil War days. But as a sort of musical organizer, he helped those in the early student sit-in movements to use music with greater effectiveness. After a while, students quite unaware of Guy Carawan, or their implicit debt to him, were singing songs he had helped to popularize. His strong role cannot be emphasized enough, although many, including this writer, lost focus on this at one point.

Carawan and his wife Candie have documented the twin Southern arms of music in the life of the everyday life of the Southern Negro in *We Shall Overcome!* (Oak) and *Ain't You Got a Right to the Tree of Life?*

(Simon and Schuster). These books speak more eloquently than any comment that could be made here.

The infectious quality of the singing has not affected only Negroes. Police Chief Pritchett, although saying that "their singing

Bessie Jones and the Georgia Sea Island Singers, 1964

Mrs. Pearly Brown, Bukka White, Rev. Pearly Brown, and Howlin' Wolf, 1966

185

is a method to incite them," added, "These people got a lot of feeling and rhythm. I enjoy hearing them sing. The songs are catchy."

With a strange detachment, Chief Pritchett described this episode of December, 1961: After more than 260 persons were booked in a mass arrest, his jail guards were singing and humming songs along with the prisoners!

Similarly, in a Charlotte (N.C.) sit-in meeting of CORE, a policeman was observed singing along, "before he caught himself." Guards in the Mississippi State Prison in Parchman have been observed doing the same. A jailer in Americus, Georgia, was said to have requested a song from a Negro prisoner. A white piano-player in Albany was heard changing the lyrics of "When the Saints Go Marching In" to "When the King [Dr. King] Comes Marching In."

There are, of course, stories to the contrary: In Dawson, Georgia, singing was forbidden in jail. In Camilla, Georgia, a prisoner was allegedly slapped for singing. In Rock Hill, South Carolina, a group was put into solitary confinement until they stopped their protests in music.

The bright strand of music in Negro life is inextricably woven into the fabric of religious tradition. A member of the Southern Regional Council emphasized the importance of the church to all rural Southerners, while the Rev. Oliver W. Holmes, associate director of the Georgia Council on Human Relations, remarked: "The smaller the community, the more important the church."

Albany, Georgia, a good example of this, had a population of 57,000, with fifty white churches and thirty Negro churches. In the congregations of the poorer, less sophisticated Negroes, some preachers use even today a form of song-sermon, which Northern folk-music fans may know at first hand from the performance of the Rev. Gary Davis.

The old techniques of the fundamentalist ministers is a form of music in itself, whether dealing in "sin, hellfire, and brimstone," or in Dr. King's "social gospel," voter registration, or "new religion of freedom."

Part of this stems from a West-African ritual tradition of call and response, and part of it fits in with the white revivalist camp-meeting pattern. Both use the phrasing, the

The Dixie Hummingbirds, 1966

Ed Young and the Southern Fife and Drum Corps, 1965

Bettie Mae Fikes, 1966

187

188

Harlem street, 1965

189

Freedom Singers, 1963

hoots, moans, and hums of music. Both use the cadences and rhythms of church song. Anyone who has watched the manner of some professional gospel singers "preaching into" their songs will know this ebb and flow of speech and song.

"Testifying" in a Negro folk church or praise-house has been likened to the more sophisticated practice of group therapy in its ability to relieve frustrations. "Getting happy" to gospel music or preaching is often a semi-hysterical seizure of fervor. As the intensity of the sermon grows, the worshippers may reply to the pulpit: "That's right," "Jesus will fix it," "Amen, brother." The degree of rapport between leader and congregation is astonishing.

Two of the young activists intensely linked with music who became well known in the folk movement were Bernice Johnson and Cordell Reagon. Bernice has a deep, booming, soaringly intense voice that reminded many of us of Odetta's, while Cordell was the absolutely tireless battler whose energy and purpose made a lot of the Northern folk liberals look a bit weak. Cordell organized a group called The Freedom Singers, which gave many concerts and raised thousands of dollars for the Student Non-Violent Coordinating Committee.

"Songs are easy," Cordell explained. "A lot we make up as we go, mostly in jail. We were sitting around a drugstore today and I made up a song in rock 'n' roll style. But the movement is constantly on people's minds. First they sing rock 'n' roll, and then they go into these freedom songs."

Encountering such dedicated young civil rights workers, who used music as their medium and their message, was a fabulous expe-

190

Freedom Singers and Guy Carawan, 1963

Len Chandler, 1965

Bettie Mae Fikes, 1966

Fannie Lou Hamer, 1965

191

Peter, Paul and Mary, Joan Baez, Bob Dylan, The Freedom
Singers, and Pete Seeger, 1963

Freedom Singers at Newport, 1964

Bernice Reagon, 1965

rience. It formed a great contrast with the middle-class youth of the Northern folk-music movement, who were, of course, trying to "say something" through their music also. But the one group was clearly involved in a day-to-day battle for its very future while the battle in the North was not so clear-cut, not so immediate, and more in the manner of a philosophical-ethical battle than a life-or-death battle.

Guy Carawan moved on from the integration movement to study and work with another sort of Negro community altogether, the ancient folk culture in the Sea Islands of Georgia and South Carolina. There, songs that had been sung before the Civil War were still an active tradition. From there came such wonderful performers as Bessie Jones and the Georgia Sea Island Singers and, from Mississippi, Ed Young and his brothers, whose bass drum and fife African-survival primitivism was strongly impressive.

194

Texas Work Song Group, 1965

All these music and life styles vary as much, from The Staples to Bessie Jones to Bernice Johnson to the Young Brothers, as do the individual styles of city revival folk song. One cannot say of this wonderful cornucopia of song that one style is any better than another, that one is more important than another. Too often have commentators on American folk song been over-concerned with definition, longevity, and evaluations of social worth. Whether the music is made as self-expression or commercial expression, there is so much to be amazed at, so much to appreciate, that it is parlous to waste time in comparative evaluation. It is just different, that is all.

What the whole range of gospel, freedom, and religious songs out of America's Negro communities does add up to, though, is a powerful chorus of great voices. Some voices are propagandizing for social change, while others are propagandizing for equality or for religious salvation or just seeking solace. Taken together, it is one of the crowning ornaments of American folk song. Taken together, it is one of the keystones of our folk music edifice.

195

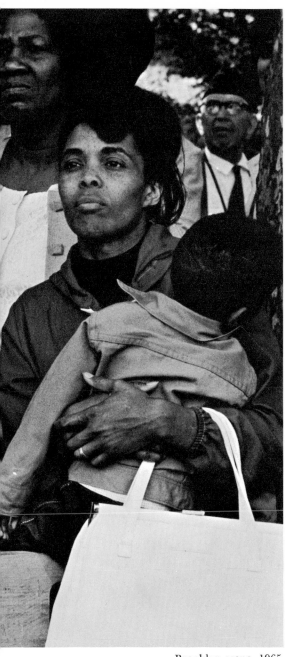

Brooklyn scene, 1965

New York City girl

VI   BIG SOUND

FROM THE COUNTRY

Where does folk music end and commercial country music take over? We pose the question, but can offer no simple answer.

The whole body of American folk and pop music is such a thickly woven mesh that certain styles are continually crossing and recrossing other styles. Nowhere is this interweave more evident than in the music generally associated with Nashville, the music loosely called "Country and Western."

A good many performers in the forty-year history of Country and Western music began as "folk performers." Some never left the precincts of folk music, while others are continually walking both sides of the musical street, changing their choice of performing style for a given song or instrumental.

Contemporary Country and Western music has changed so much, has become so sophisticated, that it is difficult to recall that nearly all of it was born in folk-oriented style. Many of the white folk performers discussed and pictured in Chapter II were to later "cross over" into the patently more commercial style of

Country and Western. Yet the majority of Bluegrass performers to be discussed here remained solidly in the center of the bridge that connects folk tradition with present-day Nashville music.

There has been an unfortunate tug-of-war between those folk fans who regard Country and Western music as an area for their study and enjoyment and those who make minute distinctions between what is pure folk and what is "corrupted" or commercial.

It is this sort of élitist approach toward folk

music and its peripheral expressions that has retarded the folk movement's ability to stay in touch with greater parts of the population. Ethnic snobs and traditional determinists think, with much persuasive argumentation on their side, that "their" music is superior. At the same time, they are denying themselves the vast excitements and stimulations of kindred and tangential musics, which, while not "pure" have much else to commend themselves.

All this by way of introduction to the lively world of Nashville music. Nashville is the capital of an international music industry. It has become the vortex of a recording, publishing, broadcasting, and personal-appearance network that spreads around the world. Nashville is know by many nicknames: Music City, U.S.A.; Tin Pan Valley; the Capital of Country Music. Nashville is not only the world center of what has become a $100,000,000-a-year country music industry, but it is also a recording center for a lot of other pop musics, a center now rivaling the supremacy of New York and Hollywood in range of activity and number of musicians and recordings involved.

As to country music, the size of its international audience is almost impossible to calculate. If we say that there are some 35,000,000 country fans in the United States and Canada, what total can be supplied when we add Britain, Ireland, Australia, Scandinavia, Germany, South Africa and Japan? To be conservative about it, let's say fifty million deep-dyed fans of country music, many of whom would be folk fans if some of the folk leaders didn't persist in keeping their music "élite" and of such arid delimitations as to allow no mass appeal.

At any rate, out of Nashville spin some 15,000 live performances annually. There are about five hundred song-writers living in the Nashville-Davidson County district, and the more than two dozen recording studios there are kept busy, often on a round-the-clock basis.

How did the industry happen to center itself in Nashville? The answer can be given in

Kilby Snow, 1966

three little words: "Grand Ole Opry." This unbelievably indestructible American radio show and institution, born November 28, 1925, was to provide the nucleus for the entire country music industry. With ever-traveling performers making the rounds, it was only their return to Nashville to appear on station WSM's "Opry" that made them available for recording.

The announcer-host of the WSM "Barn Dance," the show that was to evolve into "Grand Ole Opry," was a former newspaper man named George D. Hay, who had earlier helped station WLS in Chicago start its "Barn Dance." The performers on that first WSM show were an eighty-year-old bearded fiddler named Uncle Jimmy Thompson and his niece,

Eva Thompson Jones, who played piano and sang. Uncle Jimmy scraped out an hour's worth of old jigs, reels, and sentimental parlor and country songs. After only a few minutes, requests began to pour into the station from listeners by wire and telephone. The new show was a hit.

Just two years later, George Hay, known widely by his nickname, "The Solemn Old Judge," renamed the show 'Grand Ole Opry," and it has since become the grand old dinosaur of American radio. Having missed airtime only during a few of President Franklin D. Roosevelt's "Fireside Chats," the "Opry" is believed to be the oldest continuous broadcast in radio. Either directly on its clearchannel station or through subsidiary syndi-

Grandpa Jones and Mrs. Jones, 1967

cated shows, the country music on the "Opry" reaches some 10,000,000 persons each week.

When the "Opry" started, country music was also in its early phases. Mostly, it was just a rural folk music, put onto early radio to fill the vacuum for entertainment for regional audiences. Folk-country music was beginning to score with the simultaneous growth of electric recording. (The first country recording *of consequence* was Fiddling John Carson's Atlanta sessions of 1923.) As ironic as it may seem, it was two electronic media, recording and radio, that were to transform a regional folk music into an international industry.

The content of a four-hour "Opry" broadcast today or the infinite variety of music recorded in Nashville reflect how comprehen-

Morris Brothers, 1963

(Below) Glenn Ohrlin, 1964

(Right) Jack Elliott, Virginia and Almon Manes, 1966

Dewey Shepherd, 1964

205

Jim and Jessie McReynolds, 1966

The Greenbriar Boys, 1964

Stanley Brothers, 1964

Doc Watson, 1964

sive the term "country music" has become. It includes ballads, heart songs, Bluegrass, Western songs, train songs, breakdowns, fiddle and guitar tunes, hoedowns, and a lot more. Country music embraces a wide range of styles, from the strictly traditional folk-oriented to bright, urbane love ballads or novelty or sacred tunes that have a distinctly modern flavor. As in jazz and pop music, there are such a variety of styles and approaches to Country and Western music that each have their strong adherents.

1964

Eck Robertson, 1965

Fiddling contest at Newport, 1966

As I wrote in *The Country Music Story* (Bobbs-Merrill), the soundtrack of a documentary on country music would carry a symphony of varied sounds:

"It would be the clang of an electric guitar, the subtle fretting of Merle Travis's unamplified guitar; the piercing, stirring "Gloryland March" of Wilma Lee and Stoney Cooper; the yodeling of Kenny Roberts; the devilish banjo tricks of Don Reno; the clunk of Stringbean's old banjo; Pappy McMichen's bow sliding across his 1723 Italian violin, which he has to

Lilly Brothers, 1965

Chet Parker, 1964

Eck Robertson and Sam McGee, 1965

Mandolin Workshop, 1966

Jimmy Driftwood and son, 1959

Roger Sprung, 1963

Rosalie Sorrels, 1966

Dewey Shepherd, a friend,
and Gaither Carlton, 1964

Fiddlers at Newport, 1966

New York Ramblers, 1964

Mike Hudak and Jim Snow, 1966

John Burke, 1968

Ben Hardon, Emmy Lou Harris, and Guy Phillips, 1968

Dave Dudley, 1967

New Lost City Ramblers, 1963

209

Oliver Smith, 1966

call a fiddle; Johnny Cash pointing his guitar at an audience as if he were going to hold them up; a screaming "Howdy" from beneath Cousin Minnie Pearl's straw hat; Jimmy Wakely singing to his horse; Zeke Clements explaining how to skin a cat to make a banjo; Archie Campbell telling a racy story one minute and singing a gospel song the next; Ralph Peer telling rustic auditioners to relax and sing out in a Southern hotel room; Ernest Tubb speaking like a benign Lincoln in a ten-gallon hat; Hank Williams crying his lonesome words into a microphone; Jimmie Rodgers hearing a whistle in the night. It is a rare and exciting sound."

It would be next to impossible to compress my history of Country and Western music into one essay for this book. All that can be hinted at, for the urban folk fan, is that there is a tremendous amount of musical quality lying over the hills to Nashville. There is also a lot

of junk, pap, commercial garbage. The student or fan of Country and Western music, therefore, has a greater job of selectivity to tread between the dross and the ore. But it is worth the effort, if only to catch one of the heartfelt gospel songs of Roy Acuff, the "king of country music"; to marvel at the guitar virtuosity of Chet Atkins; to sense the beautiful part-singing of The Blue Sky Boys; to watch Cousin Emmy's dynamic manner on stage; to roar at the unhusked corn of Homer and Jethro or Grandpa Jones.

Too many thousands of performers make up the vast Breughelesque canvas of America's "other popular music," Country and Western, to be touched on here. We can only urge that you try to give Country and Western another listen—to find out why Buck Owens and George Jones and their hard-driving "honky-tonk" style of singing is so popular; to sense Roger Miller's place in a continuum that

Clarence Ashley, 1963

Clayton McMichen, 1964

Cousin Emmy, 1965

Larry Older, 1965

Bill Monroe, 1963

Bill Monroe, 1965

Bill Monroe and Blue Grass Boys, 1965

places his "King of the Road" in a direct line of descent from the hobo songs of Cliff Carlisle, to see how Hank Snow and Ernest Tubb are latter-day twigs off the sturdy branch that produced Jimmie Rodgers, "the singing brakeman" and "the father of country music," way back in the mid-1920's.

One area where the folk fan seems most closely in touch with country music is that large overlapping zone called Bluegrass. Thanks to the popularizing of such city stalwarts as Mike Seeger and Ralph Rinzler, Bluegrass is widely known to nearly every folk fan. Here is a style of rural ensemble music-making, vocal and instrumental, that is almost an equivalent of rural string-band jazz, and an equally compelling cousin of the varied instrumental bands of European and Latin-American villages.

To tell it in its simplest outlines, Bluegrass evolved from the string bands who were active

1965

213

Kentucky Colonels, 1964

Coon Creek Girls, 1966

Mac Wiseman, 1963

Sam and Kirk McGee and Arthur
Smith (fiddler), 1965

214

Johnny Cash, 1964

Midge Rice, 1965

Earl Scruggs and Lester Flatt, 1959

215

Ora Watson, 1966

Mike Seeger with Buck Graves, 1966

Phipps Family, 1964

216

Country Gentlemen, 1962

(Below) Phoeba Parsons, 1964

Charles River Valley Boys, 1965

(Left) John Cohen, Cousin Emmy, and Mike Seeger, 1965

Jim Rooney, Lue Berline, Byron Berline, and Bill Keith, 1965

217

Galax String Band or Camp Creek Boys, 1967

Sara Carter and Maybelle Carter, 1967

in the 1910's and 1920's. These string bands, such as Gid Tanner and The Skillet Lickers, had, in turn, evolved from earlier banjo-fiddle combinations of the nineteenth century. Even that trend can be found to have been an American variant of Irish and Scottish pipe and flute ensembles. Whatever this circuitous line of descent, Bluegrass style as we know it today, was largely set in the late 1940's by a series of seminal bands led by the great Kentucky singer and mandolin player, Bill Monroe.

Monroe's bands were to be the seed-bed of Bluegrass. Through its various formations passed nearly every major Bluegrass stylist of our time. The leading offshoot of Monroe's Bluegrass Boys were Lester Flatt and Earl Scruggs, whose own band, The Foggy Mountain Boys, have in their own time become the nation's leading "glamour" Bluegrass band. Scruggs's virtuosity on the five-string banjo is, of course, legendary and actual at the same time. He gave the instrument a fluidity and lyricism that was almost unknown before, and

218

Dock Boggs, 1963

Tex Logan, 1965

Mike Seeger and Maybelle Carter, 1965

Jimmie Tarlton and Mike Seeger, 1966

his style of picking has been widely imitated.

During the height of the urban folk revival, there were to be nearly as many excellent city-based Bluegrass bands as there were in the country. As with country bands, the urban pickers generally kept the same instrumentation of guitar, banjo, mandolin, Dobro (a steel guitar fretted in the Hawaiian manner), and bass. The voices were to be as athletic and free as were the instruments, with the over-all sound adding up to a kind of whirlwind magic. Among the best of the city bands are The Greenbriar Boys and The Charles River Valley Boys, New Yorkers and Bostonians respectively, who added country-born members and went on to become important style-setters in the folk revival.

Of course, to single out just a few country and city Bluegrass bands scarcely does justice to the breadth of this important subdivision of American folk and country music. But for the person seeking an introduction to one of the more exciting musical styles of our era, the recordings of these groups would speak volumes.

The debate about whether to consider all of Country and Western music as part of the folk stream will not end overnight. What is clear is that a growing catholicity of taste is happily spreading through the folk movement, beginning to embrace neighboring musical styles that have esthetic validity, if not purity. It is in this spirit that the work of the John Edwards Memorial Foundation at the University of California at Los Angeles is to be praised.

Here is a study and research center devoted generally to American folk music, but specifically to the Country and Western field. It is the hope of many of us who regard Country and Western as a viable field for study, that the Edwards Foundation will prosper and grow. It appears to be the reigning philosophy of many at the foundation that Hank Williams is as worthy of study as is The Texas Drifter, Goebel Reeves; that Johnny Cash is at least as important as some unkown folk minstrel who never made a cent commercially, but who stuck stubbornly to his own native tradition. It is such approaches as this that

220

Osborne Brothers, 1964

Sara Carter, 1967

Ollie Gilbert and Jimmy Driftwood, 1964

French Carpenter, Roscoe and Phoeba Parsons, 1964

French Carpenter and Jenes Cottell, 1963

Tony Glover's boots, 1965

223

Michael Gorman, 1965

make one feel that the folk movement in the United States is really coming of age, beginning to understand that there are popular musics of value even though they do not measure up to the rigorous standards of a purely traditional esthetic.

But while apreciating this, one must also have respect for the tireless proponents of the older music. In this regard, one can have nothing but praise for such groups as The Friends of Old-Time Music, a small and definitely non-profit organization that brought to New York and many other cities of the Northeast the very best in obscure country musicians. Working independently at first, and later cooperating with the Newport Folk Foundation, the Friends of Old-Time Music were trying to say that the folk musicians who had been passed over by Nashville had as much to say, in human and musical terms, as any star turned out by Country and Western music.

Michael Gorman, 1965

The hands of Jean Ritchie, 1963

Sylvia Tyson's hands, 1965

225

The musical-revival trio The New Lost City Ramblers was also trying to spread the wonder and magic of string-band music of the 1920's and 1930's with its own playing. Soon, The New Lost City Ramblers were themselves losing work to the musicians they had helped rediscover from the past. The success of The Ramblers ironically worked to make the music and musicians they studied come to the fore while the group that had done this so painstakingly was actually receding quietly into oblivion. This selfless form of activity repre-

sents perhaps one of the glowing, little-known aspects of the folk revival that gave it beauty and ethics and honor.

In the face of those for whom the folk revival was either just a vehicle to peddle their own wares, their own dogma, or their own egos, The work of The Friends of Old-Time Music and The New Lost City Ramblers will help remind everyone of what the best impulses were among the city youngsters who helped produce the folk revival of yesterday, today, and tomorrow.

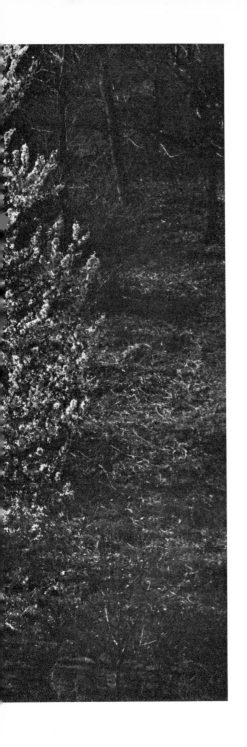

VII   MANY FACES

OF THE BLUES

*People, if you hear me humming on this song
    both night and day,
People, if you hear me humming on this song
    both night and day,
I'm just a poor boy in trouble, trying to drive
    those blues away . . .*

If any pattern can be found in the crazy patchwork that is American popular musical taste, it is the pattern of repetition. The cycles of return can scarcely be plotted or graphed in a scientific fashion, but we are always returning to a music of the past, often with a modern face.

The cyclical inevitability that governs so much in American popular music is nowhere more evident than with the blues, a bedrock native form that crops out again and again in its pristine form or in forms that have gone through as many metamorphoses as the earth upon which we live.

During the heat of the folk revival of the 1960's, the blues were everywhere. The simple old plaints of rural Negroes were enjoying

230

their biggest vogue in two decades. The songs of sweat and sorrow and solace were being recorded again by the hundreds. Old-time performers not known outside their home locales were appearing increasingly before large city audiences as far from home as Paris.

The blues has many faces. It is big-band music, hot and swinging, a base for dancing. It is also a sophisticated composer, Harold Arlen, being "Happy With the Blues," and an opera star, Eileen Farrell, recording "I've Got a Right to Sing the Blues."

Street musicians, 1966

But before we get to those polished latter-day images of the blues, let's talk about where it all started, the folk blues or country blues, that earthy, shirtsleeve-basic music language that translated feeling into melody. Take, for example, this lyric from the singing of rediscovered blues man Sleepy John Estes:

You know, them rats is mean in my kitchen,
I've ordered
me a mountain cat, (twice)
You know, the way they's 'stroying my groceries,
boys,
I declare it's tóugh like that.
You know, I've got five little children, boys,
On my disability check, (three times) ,
You know, I got to go back and check with my
worker, boys,
On account of those dogonne rats . . .

Are the rats that plagued the childhood of Richard Wright's *Native Son* any more graphically described in that novel than the rats that infested the life of Sleepy John Estes? This is the main face of the blues—personal experience translated directly into song. The blues can be happy, can dance, can even become elegant and stately, polished and sophisticated. But they started with rats in the kitchen.

An entire portrait of Negro life in America could be drawn through the lyrics of country and folk blues. Such a portrait, which admittedly dwelled upon the poverty-stalked side of life, has been drawn masterfully by the British blues authority Paul Oliver in *Blues Fell This Morning: The Meaning of the Blues* (Horizon Press) .

Oliver's study is both a source of wonderment and shame, a document of evil drawn in bold strokes, a musical-sociological masterpiece that is, not surprisingly, the work of an Englishman. (Until recently, the British knew more about American blues that did white America, an incongruous situation that is now happily changing.) Oliver used the easel of blues lyrics on which to draw a realistic, compassionate canvas of an oppressed people.

Although the social conditions that gave rise to the blues may be changing dramati-

Memphis Slim, 1960

cally, they still fester in the deep South and in the Negro ghettoes of the North. Behind the beat and the cry of the blues is a message about social disorganization and suffering. Because the white majority began to tune in on the message of the Negroes in the civil rights movement of the 1960's, the blues can be said to have an even greater urgency and immediacy than they ever had.

Whatever impact the many able white city interpreters of the blues have made in the last few years, it is still the Southern Negro blues performer who must be regarded as the keeper of the grand tradition. So many fine old blues men have been "unearthed," "rediscovered," or "discovered" since the late 1950's that one must be wary about the continuing use of the slogan that "such and such is the last of the great country blues performers."

With the inroads of mass communication and the shift in cultural values of rural Negroes, there is much evidence to indicate that the old country blues tradition is ebbing. Still, one recalls the laments of the English folksong collectors at the end of the last century who said that the rural tradition had died with the industrial revolution.

But the alarms of the conservatives in folk song, of whom there are many (even if they fly the banner of radicalism), are probably without foundation. The existence of a folk arts revival in the midst of a period of unparalleled American prosperity promises as

Mary Travers, 1964

Brownie McGhee, 1959

much for the continuance of a country blues tradition as for the continuance of the Spanish *cante hondo*, the Rumanian *doina* and the Portuguese *fado*. The blues will die when personal unhappiness dies. Folk art has nothing if not durability.

So, it seems, do the old-time blues men. Sam (Lightning) Hopkins is in his sixties; Sleepy John Estes and the Rev. Gary Davis, a "holy blues" man, are in their seventies. There are, of course, many examples of blues men whose hard lives ended early—Leroy Carr, Big Bill Broonzy, and Blind Lemon Jefferson all died before their time. However, particularly rug-

Brownsville, Brooklyn, 1963

234

(Right) Ed Young and the Southern Fife and Drum Corps, 1965

(Below) Brother John Sellers, 1962

Sleepy John Estes, 1964

Little Brother Montgomery, 1960

Jesse Fuller, 1964

235

ged constitutions have seemingly given added years to such men as Furry Lewis and Mance Lipscomb, Memphis Willie B. (Borum) and Tampa Red, Lonnie Johnson and a woman blues singer who rolls on like the Mississippi, Victoria Spivey.

Even within the precincts of one such generalized style as folk or country blues, there was a stylist for every taste. Mississippi John Hurt was the sweet-voiced, gentle bluesman and songster. We have spoken of him earlier. Skip James, with his high and keening voice, could carve his initials on your memory on only one hearing. Big Joe Williams, blustery and bold, driving out with energy, as would a turbulent talent such as Bukka White. Son James, perhaps still the reigning "king of the country blues," was rediscovered later than all, and yet he may have stylistically been as important as any blues singer since Robert Johnson. Blind Snooks Eaglin, rasping out his streetcorner shouts. Roosevelt Sykes, spreading a kind of rollicking honey over the blues at his piano. Memphis Slim and Willie Dixon, professionals to a fault, knowing how to whip up the audience with a beat. Robert Pete Williams sang his way out of Louisiana State Prison at Angola (once Leadbelly's home jail), winning his parole through the pledge of his musical talent. John Lee Hooker, quiet and monosyllabic offstage, suddenly became an articulate bard when he had a guitar in his hands, with his moody, introspective world coming through in dozens of tunes. Sonny Terry and Brownie McGhee were old-timers who had been big in the first folk revival of World War II and went right on with their great musical dialogues.

The list of great folk blues men is so long and so distinguished that one can only marvel at the infinite variety of the blues and the seemingly limitless potential of such a simple form. Whether it is the bottleneck guitar fretting of a Fred McDowell or the clarion harmonica of Sonny Boy Williamson II or the suave, amiable sophistication of Josh White, each of the great stylists had his own way of speaking to and through the blues. It was a universal language with a thousand dialects.

Mance Lipscomb, 1965

236

The Rodriguez Brothers, 1964

Robert Pete Williams, 1964

Robert Pete Williams, 1964

Leonda, 1967

Jesse Fuller, 1964

Muddy Waters, 1964

Muddy Waters at guitar, Otis Spann and the Blues Band, 1967

Muddy Waters, Barbara Dane, and Tom Clancy, 1964

Rev. & Mrs. Gary Davis, 1965

Staple Singers, 1967

238

Fuzzy Lewis, 1963

Fuzzy Lewis, Gus Cannon, and Memphis
Willie B., 1963

Memphis Willie B., 1963

Gus Cannon, 1963

Bill Lee, 1966

Mississippi John Hurt, 1965

Although tastes in blues men could vary widely, a few of the best could cut across all lines. Such a performer was the Texas "find," Sam (Lightning) Hopkins. Reviewing a concert by Hopkins at The Village Gate in October, 1960, I felt as if this was certainly the symbolic country blues man who best typified what the blues revival was all about:

"The many faces of trouble provided the raw material for yesterday afternoon's concert by Sam (Lightning) Hopkins.

"The Texas country blues singer's highly personal songs told of love unfulfilled and devotion unappreciated. He transformed such blunt complaints as 'Have you ever been mistreated?' into artistic statements with his voice and guitar.

"Although Mr. Hopkins' sentiments may be primary, their expression is not. Trouble was treated sardonically, with broad humor and pathos. The blues form may seem simple and limiting, but at the hands of a master they burgeoned into a subtle exploration of moods.

"Mr. Hopkins was giving a solo program, but his guitar frequently suggested another voice, which sometimes replied to or ended his vocal phrases.

"Apparently much more relaxed than he had been at his Carnegie Hall appearance earlier this month, Mr. Hopkins was able to match his inner feelings with moving, lowering singing."

So it was with the country bluesmen, having their brief hour of glory on the American stage. Many of them continued to struggle to make a living, despite a dozen recordings on such specialist labels as Arhoolie, Delmark, or the indefatigable Bluesville series on Prestige. Many of them were really popular in Britain, West Germany, and France in the early 1960's, single-handedly drawing greater and hipper audiences than they did here in America. The

240

Juanita Hall, 1962

Bukka White, 1966

John Lee Hooker, 1963

spread of the American blues to Europe was to start another sort of music revolution, one subsequently felt over here. But the irony was that the seminal blues men still led lives of unalloyed trouble. Discrimination against their color was a problem they had little escape from. Their economic plight was only briefly relieved by the clamor for blues in this country and Western Europe. The blues did what they could to drive the trouble away, and because the trouble returned, so too did the music it produced and alleviated.

241

Howling Wolf, 1966

Chambers Brothers, 1965

Big Joe Williams, 1966

Willie Dixon, 1961

Willie Dixon and Eddie Boyd, 1965

The Chambers Dancers, 1967

Ian and Sylvia, 1965

Skip James, 1964

Judy Roderick, 1964

Eric Von Schmidt, 1963

Fred McDowell, 1964

245

Preservation Hall Band, 1966

(Left) George Lewis, 1966

(Right) Billie Pierce, 1966

After the blues left its rural birthplace, after the forms that had sired the blues—the spiritual and the holler—had lost their grasp on tradition, the blues changed dramatically in style. For this transition, a whole new set of standards for the listener had to be developed. On one hand, the blues went to the city and became sophisticated—brasher and more extroverted. On the other, white singers came to love the simple, conversational ease of talking in the blues song, and we had an entire new school of bluesmen. As is too often typical of the immaturities of the folk movement, this change was something without any past yardsticks to measure, and contention set in. The law-makers of folk purism got themselves unnecessarily tangled up because some elements of the blues had changed in becoming urbanized, and, tragedy of all tragedies, there were white men singing Negro music, some even making a living at it!

Well, I am not going to waste space doing

246

battle with the hardheads who simply couldn't readjust to the concept of the blues as a living musical organism bound and destined to go through change. They have missed out on one of the great musical revolutions of our time, and have, with their doctrinal confusion, simply deafened themselves to a lot of excellent performances.

Perhaps no single performer better represents the change from country to city blues than Muddy Waters. This first-rate singer had been recorded for the Library of Congress in the World War II period. Those recordings are available from the Archive of American Folk Song and on an excellent commercial re-issue on Pete Welding's Testament label. At that time, Waters name was Mackinley Morganfield, and his style was close to the Missis-sippi Delta, a tightly personal, introverted style.

But he was to go North, to find a living in the clubs of Chicago's steaming South Side. Naturally, Muddy's music changed with his new life, his new environment. What emerged was a bolder style, with full and heavy instru-mentation, electric guitars and basses; hard-driving, pungent harmonicas, amplifiers, mi-crophones, and drums. It was a city music, linked to the sound of the auto horn, the street-car, the cabaret. But the core of the blues as a life-style music persisted. All the old aches and pains were there, but the method of describing them and treating them had changed.

From such post-war transitional figures as Muddy Waters emerged a new style of music,

Son House, 1965

Lightning Hopkins, 1965

Ed Paine. PHOTO BY JULIUS LESTER

The hands of Lightning Hopkins, 1965

Sippie Wallace, 1967

long described in the music trade papers as "rhythm and blues." It was to prove enormously popular with urban Negro audiences, deeply affected the stylistic growth of gospel, and played an ever-growing role in the history of jazz. Rhythm and blues was increasingly to play a great role with white city audiences, but in a most surprising way.

That way was rock 'n' roll, or to give some of its other euphemisms, big-beat music or pop. The surprise of the 1960's was that it was largely Negro music going to Britain, catching fire with young English groups and then rico-

Donovan, 1965

the sound, face and mind of today
is more relative to the hope of tomorrow
and the reality of destruction
than the blind who cannot see
their children for fear and division.
something that grew and related
ive reflections of today's children...... THE ROLLIN

cheting back here. Negro rhythm and blues had had its first major influence on American pop music in the 1950's when several country singers, notably Elvis Presley, Carl Perkins, and Bill Haley, were to synthesize a style out of country elements and rhythm and blues. The first white rock 'n' roll craze ran from about 1955 until 1960. In the latter year, the music industry was wracked with several "payola" scandals. A general revulsion against rock 'n' roll set in, generalizing, with considerable unfairness, that rock and payola and blaring music were all one and the same.

It was during the first nadir of rock 'n' roll that folk music's current revival set in so strongly. There were overtones of a reaction, in which the somewhat seedy world of rock 'n' roll of the late 1950's needed an antidote, and the idealistic anti-commercialism of folk song worked perfectly, as we have seen. But, contrary to the recurring prophesies that rock 'n' roll was dead, the youth of Britain had

252

Country Joe and the Fish, 1968

Dave Van Ronk, 1964

The Fugs, 1965

The Fugs, 1965

254

The Blues Project, 1966

The Fugs, 1965

DYLAN 4 EVER

Bob Dylan, 1965

Bob Dylan and Albert Grossman, 1965

Bob Dylan, Donovan, and Mary Travers, 1965

some other ideas. A whole school of young Liverpool musicians, notably The Beatles, were fascinated with the recordings of such rhythm and blues exponents as Little Richard, Muddy Waters, and The Everly Brothers.

From these influences, British rock was born in the early 1960's. The race was on, and scores of groups, such as The Rolling Stones, The Dave Clark Five, The Animals and many others began to perform rhythm and blues with an English accent. In many cases, the Britons seemed to understand what American blues were all about better than American

Bob Dylan, 1965

Bob Dylan, 1965

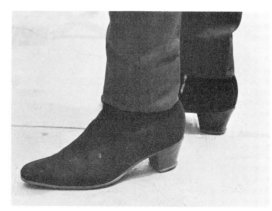

Bob Dylan, 1965

Bob Dylan's boots, 1965

white musicians. In not very much time, the so-called "British Invasion" brought it all back home, to use Bob Dylan's felicitous phrase. Largely unaware of our own great blues tradition, the American mass audience took to rhythm and blues in its English style as they had never taken to American performers. The discotheque rage was almost simultaneous, and soon we had as strong a big-beat culture as did the British.

For a time, the folk vigilantes were concerned lest this all add up to a culture-theft. But the fears again were groundless. The

257

Tim Hardin, 1966

British rock phenomenon of the 1960's only helped to stimulate tremendous interest there and throughout Western Europe in American Negro blues of all sorts, from down-home to Chicago to Detroit. Soon, traveling American Negro bluesmen were finding, as had Josh White and Big Bill Broonzy in the 1940's, that their music cast a magic spell in Western Europe. Prophets with all too little honor in their own land, they could, many for the first times in their lives, make a decent living by touring Europe.

By the mid-1960's there was a substantial American audience for the American rhythm and blues people, and such performers as Howling Wolf, Junior Wells, B. B. King, Chuck Berry, and other Chicago stars were stepping out as the great performers they always have been, but with a much larger audience. No longer relegated to such places as Pepper's Lounge in Chicago or Manhattan's Apollo Theater, the great stylists of rhythm and blues were being equally sought after for folk and jazz festivals. Late, pitifully late, the prophets without honor were getting the recognition they deserved.

The resurgence of the American blues had not exactly caught many folk fans by surprise. Such dauntless boosters for the blues as the field collector Sam Charters, the record col-

Harvey Brooks, 1966

Eric Andersen, 1966

Eric Andersen, 1966

Tim Hardin, 1966

lector Len Kunstadt and the record-maker Bob Koester had been shouting about the blues for years. The hippest of the city musiicans had been students of the blues for years. (Bob Dylan was proclaiming his love for Lit-

tle Richard before The Beatles had ever been heard from.)

But the success of the British rock groups in reminding us about the blues was soon to have an overwhelming impact on American

Jackson Browne, Tuli Kupferberg, Stefan Grossman, and Steve
Noonan, 1967

Tuli Kupferberg, 1967

260

The Lovin' Spoonful, 1966

Judy Collins, 1966

Mike Bloomfield, Paul Butterfield, and Sam Lay, 1965

Paul Butterfield Blues Band, 1965

263

The Fugs, 1965

folk musicians. Because of the economic insecurity of the entire pop music industry, it was understandable that the musicians would turn to the music that was prospering. When the Paul Butterfield Blues Band came East from Chicago in the winter of 1965–66, the advent of a major reorientation in folk circles was beginning. When Bob Dylan released his first full LP with electric instruments, the change started in earnest, although most people forgot his electric backing on several cuts from his second LP, "The Freewheeling Bob Dylan," also long before The Beatles.

Soon "The Beatles Backlash" was manifesting itself strongly. Out of Chicago, it nestled in Greenwich Village, then moved to the Sunset Strip, then San Francisco, and soon the blues and rock 'n' roll were omnipresent.

264

Maria D'Amato, 1964

Mel Lyman, 1965

Jim Kweskin Jug Band, 1966

Jim and Marilyn Kweskin and child, 1966

Again, Dylan made history by fusing his own poetic lyrics with a rock beat, leading to a fusion form that *Billboard* dubbed "folk rock." While the first few months of folk rock looked esthetically disastrous, with tangential performers like Barry McGuire and P.F. Sloan leading developments, soon, as it always does in even the highly commercialized precincts of our pop music, quality sorted itself out. Folk rock began to mean such artistic performers as Butterfield, Dylan, The Byrds, The Lovin' Spoonful, Janis Ian, and Simon and Garfunkel. Suddenly we found more meaning, more lyrical content, more purpose to our pop music than we ever had before.

Geoff Muldaur, 1966

268

Jim Kweskin Jug Band, 1966

The white blues performers were still fighting a kind of rear-guard action against those folk purists who again felt that Negro music should only be performed by Negro singers. Despite this, John Hammond, John Koerner, Tony Glover, Dave Ray, Fred Neil, Tim Hardin, and others were forging a new and more meaningful music of their own, however much it owed to Negro blues. Soon, folk rock at the hands of such a strong innovator as the late Richard Fariña was building a compelling

new music out of the old. The simple standards of what a city folk music "should be" were being assaulted by the magic imaginations of the folk-derived musicians, who thought only in terms of what a modern pop-folk idiom "could be."

The ideological battle waged on and on, droning off into meaningless verbal duels. The traditionalists felt themselves attacked, when in fact no one was attacking traditional music at all, they were simply adding another length,

Paul Arnoldi, 1964

John and Lorey Sebastian, 1966

David Blue, 1965

a new dimension to a contemporary folk expression. Pete Seeger, at first quite unsympathetic to the new folk-rock events, finally marked his own flexibility by cutting a record backed by the electric band, The Blues Project. Joan Baez made her love of The Beatles and rock 'n' roll quite well known. It was, as such broadminded commentators as Paul Nelson were saying, not an end to the folk revival, just a new phase of the revival, a new amalgamation of differing elements in American pop music tradition.

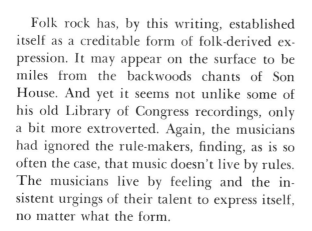

(Left) John Sebastian, Cass Elliot, and Lorey Sebastian, 1966

John Hammond, 1964

Al Kooper, 1968

Folk rock has, by this writing, established itself as a creditable form of folk-derived expression. It may appear on the surface to be miles from the backwoods chants of Son House. And yet it seems not unlike some of his old Library of Congress recordings, only a bit more extroverted. Again, the musicians had ignored the rule-makers, finding, as is so often the case, that music doesn't live by rules. The musicians live by feeling and the insistent urgings of their talent to express itself, no matter what the form.

Mimi and Richard Fariña, 1965

Richard Fariña, Joan Baez, and Mimi Fariña, 1965

Mimi Fariña, 1967

John Koerner, 1965

Koerner, Ray, and Glover, 1964

Tony Glover, 1965

Dave Ray, 1964. PHOTO BY PAUL NELSON

Lance Wakely and friend, 1966

Peter Walker, 1967

Sandy Bull, 1962

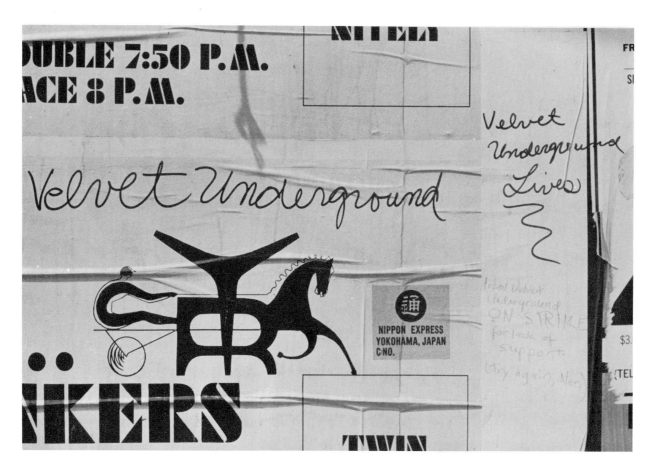

Jackson Browne, 1967

Gypsy girl

Tim Buckley, 1967.

The Blues Project, 1965

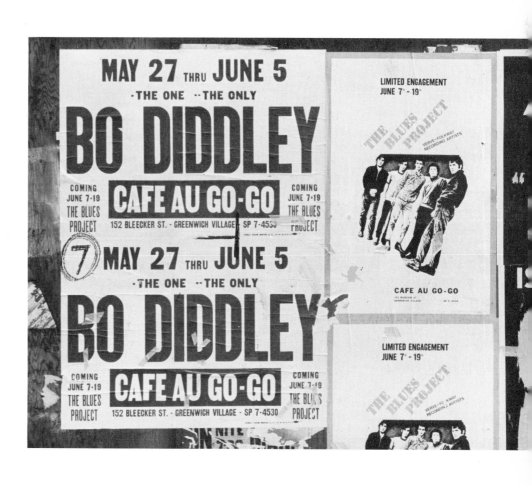

VIII   A RIVER

WITHOUT END

Ten years of super-popularity of American folk music have had a strange effect on the entire field. We now have an exceedingly sophisticated audience for a music that was originally the antithesis of sophistication.

While the folk audience is continually being replenished, from below, with new youngsters making their first voyages of discovery into new terrain, those who have been around for a few years know more about folk song in depth than did their counterparts of a few years ago.

No longer is the folk fan content with such simple songs as "I Gave My Love a Cherry." Rather, the folk fan today can be one of the most free-wheeling music-lovers to be found. Not only will he appreciate a Delta blues song and know how it differs from a Memphis soul song, but he will thrill equally to the dissonant seconds of a Bulgarian peasant girls

Guy Carawan, 1960

choir, the similarities between a Yugoslav village band and a Bluegrass country band, the similarity of an Irish pipe and fiddle combination to an American banjo-fiddle duo, and so on.

Beyond the musical values, the "sophisticated" folk fan is as deeply aware of the sociology of music as is any listener, knowing that behind every one of hundreds of world folk styles is a human enclave that works, worships, and rules itself by different standards and traditions than other groups and sub-groups. Music was never more truly a doorway to people.

This nurturing of total folk-culture appreciation developed in several ways. As we have already discussed, large squadrons of young collectors and musicians and enthusiasts "took to the hills" in a desire to get close to the music of the American countryside. Country performers became a commonplace in the city.

Then began a massive entry of foreign folk performers, mostly polished professionals, who could project from the stage their individual backgrounds and expressions. Finally, under the aegis of the Newport Folk Festival and other groups, regional festivals of folk music and folk arts were stimulated.

The importation of foreign folk music was to be, as with other areas of the folk revival, a curious mixture of show business and comparative musicology. Long before Harry Belafonte started a vogue for Calypso music, Marais and Miranda had given us some view of South African folk song through their charming songs taken from the Afrikaans. Flourishing in the 1940's, this pair may have given us only one side of African life, yet it was diverting and entertaining. Curiously, it was not until quite late in their careers that the couple began to perform songs of native black Africans.

Belafonte was to introduce to the American audience a compelling artist, Miriam Makeba, who made African tribal music alive on our stage. With glamour and stage music, Miss Makeba gave us insights into the life and the music of another side of South Africa, a side that was considerably more tempestuous, traditional, and rooted-to-life than the songs of Marais and Miranda.

Other performers from Africa, such as the Ishangi Dancers and Spokes Mashiyane, the gifted pennywhistler, showed us more of Africa's music. Withal, Africa, which some students consider to be our most musical continent, is still largely untapped by the American folk movement. While much of the really

288

ethnic music there is, perforce, limited in appeal and must remain on the recordings of the Ethnic Folkways Library and other LP's, still one can envision much more of the performing arts of Africa being imported here. The African legacy, already deeply affecting much of our Negro folk song and jazz, has still to make its massive impact on America as a performing art.

Because of the links in language and common cultural ties, the folk songs of England, Scotland, and Ireland have been widely presented in America. The British folk "invasion" long preceded the British "pop invasion," with such sterling performers as Ewan MacColl, A. L. Lloyd, Norman Kennedy, Bob Davenport, Jean Redpath, Roy Guest, Isla Cameron, Donovan, and Lou Killen.

From this incredibly diverse and gifted set of singers, we were to hear the classic ballads, the old broadsides, the work and play songs, and the latter-day topical songs. As befits the strong current of individualism in professional folk performance, we were to hear as many different views of British tradition as there were performers, from the craggy unaccompanied ballads of MacColl to the beguilingly beautiful "song of the seals" of the Scottish isles from Miss Redpath.

The fact that passport restrictions have kept important singers and thinkers such as MacColl from our shores in recent years is a poor reflection on our own immigration laws. MacColl is one of the truly important figures in world folk song, for all the cantankerousness of his theorizing and the egotism of his

Lower East Side, 1965

personality. MacColl's adventures into new forms like the "radio ballad" and mummer's plays represent the effort to incorporate folk tradition into new art forms. His sort of imagination and creativity have been sorely missed on the American scene.

Ireland, of course, with its rampant and active oral arts tradition, was to send us many

Marc Silber, 1968

290

Buffy Sainte-Marie, 1966

performers, as varied as that raspy-voiced old shouter, Margaret Barry, to those versatile singing actors, The Clancy Brothers and Tommy Makem. One aspect of the careers of Tom, Pat, and Liam Clancy and Makem is worth pondering. Originally, they left Ireland in the 1950's because of limited cultural outlets. They eased themselves into professional singing here and soon established a following of Irish-Americans even broader than their early folk following. With success established here, the three brothers and friend Makem were able to break through to the audience in Ireland. Although Ireland had a long unbroken tradition of folk song, the Clancy-Makem quartet was able to trigger a broader,

more popular revival in their own country than the folk leadership of Ireland had ever seen. Soon other groups—The Irish Rovers, The Dubliners, and others—were projecting a heavily traditional pop-folk music that had all of Ireland singing again in a louder voice than ever. Now the Clancys and Makem lead the enviable lives of jet-commuting expatriates as they return each year, like yo-yos on a short string, to their homeland after months of performing in America, Britain, and elsewhere. Along the way, they are telling the Irish a bit about American folk culture, too.

Canada has also been having its folk boom. It has sent us such singers as Alan Mills and Ian and Sylvia and such fiddle wizards as Jean

292

Chad Mitchell, 1964

Bob Davenport, 1963

Chad Mitchell Trio, 1964

293

Mike Settle, Pete Seeger, and Tom Paxton, 1963

294

Bob Dylan and Pete Seeger, 1963

Sgt. Barry Sadler, 1966

(Below) The New World Singers with Pete Seeger, 1962

Bill Thacher, 1964

Carignan. The hard-working Oscar Brand, born in Western Canada, has had an equally successful career in American and Canadian folk areas, making himself a well-known figure on the airlines between New York, Toronto, and Montreal.

An aspect of Canadian folk expression that we still know all too little about in the United States is the French chansonnier movement of Montreal, which is both a topical, nationalistic expression and a musical style. A few of their singers, such as Monique Leyrac and Claude Gauthier, have visited us, but again, with only a small geographical distance between us, we have not really heard enough of French-Canadian song.

But we don't have to go that far from native ground to find areas for the revival to explore. For years the music of the American Indian was a source of study for only the most dedicated of ethnologists and anthropologists. Because of the primitive musical form and

297

Peter Schumann of Bread and Puppet Theater, 1967

Bread and Puppet Theater, 1967

Teatro Campesino, 1967

Arlo Guthrie, 1967

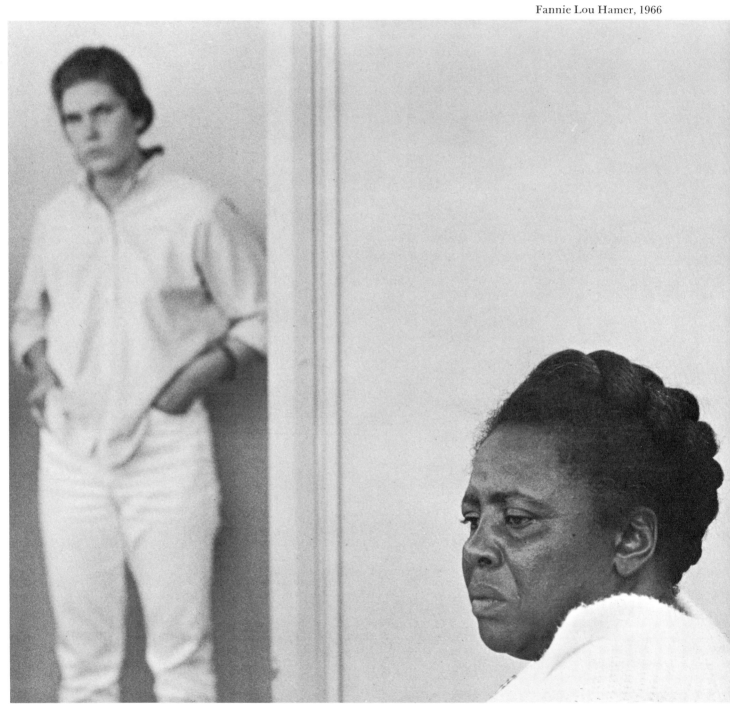

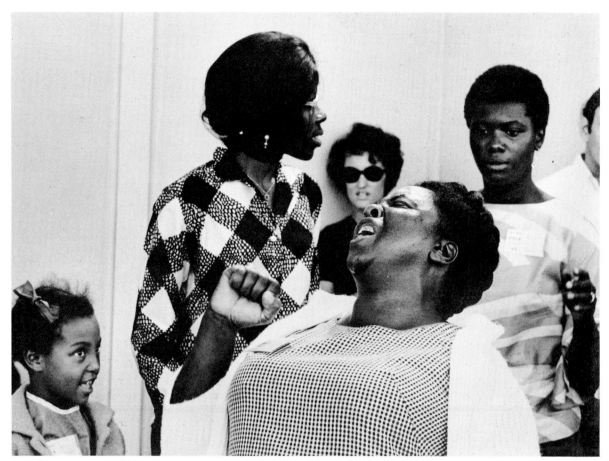

Fannie Lou Hamer, 1966

language again, many folk-revivalists simply feared to tread into this ground. A few years ago, one lively professor, David McAllester of Wesleyan University, put on a winning lecture-demonstration that helped crash the sound barrier to American Indian tradition.

Then, hand-in-hand with the rising interest in civil rights for all Americans, a new focus on Indian affairs and their shabby treatment by the white majority ushered in a brief period of Indian songs. The late Peter LaFarge wrote many songs about the miserable treatment of Indians, many of which were to be recorded by another singer of Indian descent, Johnny Cash. Buffy Sainte-Marie walked several paths at once, emerging as a popular city-bred folk singer and songwriter as well as a person deeply cognizant of her Indian background and of her debt to that background. Pat Sky and Mike Settle would sing and talk about their Indian ancestry, and helped us all to begin the massive job of refocusing our sights upon our own great primitive music (not always so primitive, one hastens to add), a treasure of still-living tradition in Indian music.

There is hope that these grass-roots will continue to be revitalized and encouraged to flower. One of the finest results of the entire Newport Folk Festival endeavor has quite little to do with the programs each summer in the Rhode Island resort city. Certain sums of money were allocated by the Newport Folk Foundation to help stimulate regional folk festivals. Thus, the Cajuns of Louisiana and the Negroes of the Carolina and Georgia Sea Islands were assisted in reappreciating their own vibrant folk cultures. As described in several reports in the Newport Festival program books, these festivals in far-off and isolated enclaves worked wonders for the morale of peoples who had felt a sense of apartness from the majority and who were gradually, almost inevitably, losing their hold on their own traditions.

Julius Lester, 1966

Bill McAdoo, 1960

Tom Paxton, 1964

304

Phil Ochs, 1965

Phil Ochs, 1965

Peter LaFarge, 1964

Mark Spoelstra, 1965

The challenge and success of these Newport-aided festivals would make an exciting document in itself. We can hope that the foundation will turn to such areas as Indian music and dozens of other minority folk cultures. It is a race against time to keep alive the spark of tradition in the face of the hurricane wind of our supermarket, paperback, TV culture. Being an optimist and reverting to the theory of cycles again, this observer feels that the race against time will be won.

The problems of folk music are not all in the country, or with minority groups, by any means. The city revival was uncovering a new problem with each new surge forward, was running into philosophical quandaries with each new step toward getting our whole country folk-oriented. Mostly, the question

308

Richard Fariña, 1965

Malvina Reynolds, 1964

(Right) Patrick Sky, 1965

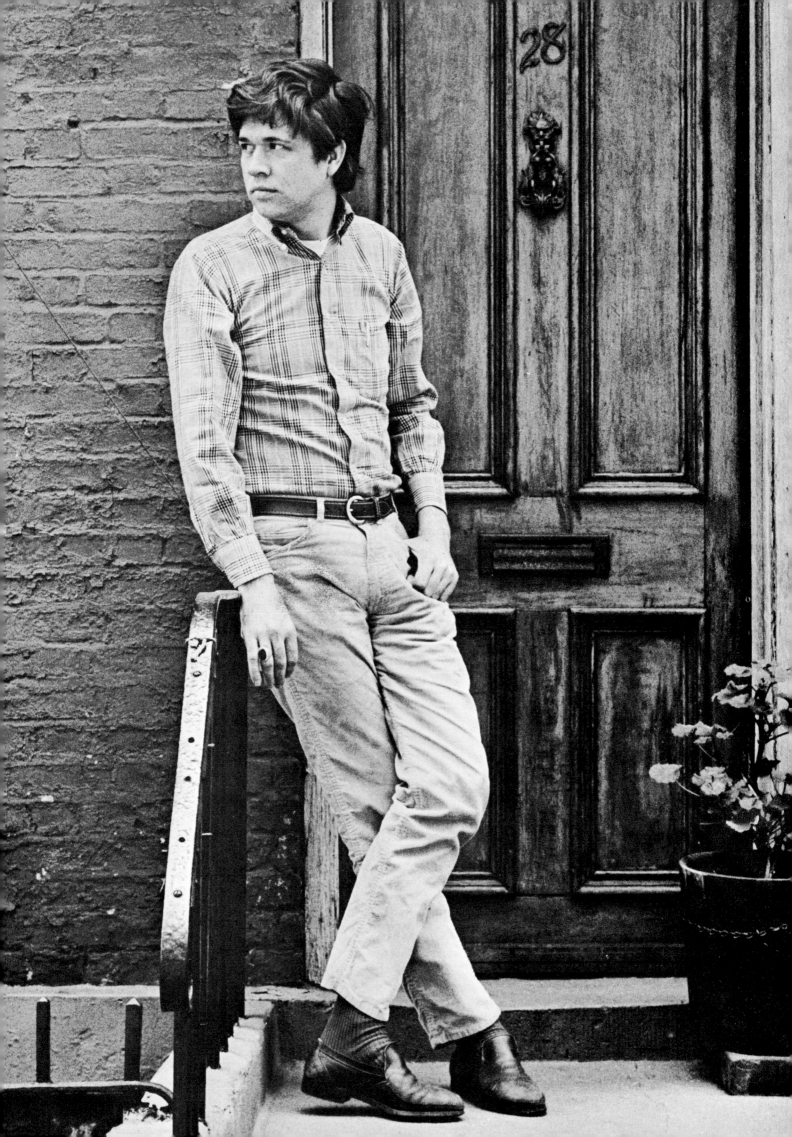

Dave Ray, 1964

314

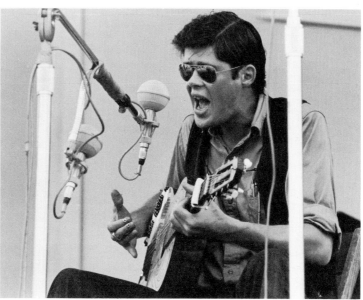

John Koerner, 1965

Pete Bellamy of Young Tradition, 1967

Carolyn Hester, 1966

Julius Lester, 1965

Jerry Jeff Walker, 1968

Phil Ochs, 1965

Tom Paxton, 1964

Eric Andersen, 1964

318

Tom Paxton, Eric Andersen, and Phil Ochs, 1964

Tim Hardin, 1966

Buffy Sainte-Marie, 1963

320

Leonard Cohen, 1967

Joni Mitchell, 1967

321

Gordon Lightfoot, 1965

Jack Elliott, 1964

322

Ian Tyson, 1965

Sylvia Tyson, 1965

Bob Dylan, 1963

Patrick Sky, 1965

Tim Buckley, 1967

Richard Fariña, 1965

Bruce Murdock, 1965　　David Blue, 1968

Simon and Garfunkel, 1968

Malvina Reynolds, 1964

Arlo Guthrie, 1967

Tom Rush, 1965

Peter LaFarge, 1963

Janis Ian, 1967

Steve Noonan, 1967

329

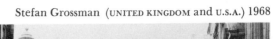
Stefan Grossman (UNITED KINGDOM and U.S.A.) 1968

Sally Angie (UNITED KINGDOM) 1968

London, 1968

330

London, 1968

The Pentangle (UNITED KINGDOM) 1968

Fiun Kalvik (NORWAY), Bert Jansch,
(UNITED KINGDOM) and Charles II

331

London, 1968

Bert Jansch, (UNITED KINGDOM) 1968

Bob Southern and Dave Brock
(UNITED KINGDOM), 1968

Norman Kennedy, Michael Gorman, A. L. Lloyd,
Margaret Barry, Annie Walters, and Arthur Nicolle,
1965 (UNITED KINGDOM and IRELAND)

Ewan MacColl (UNITED KINGDOM) and Peggy Seeger, 1960

O. J. Abbott (CANADA) and Ewan MacColl (UNITED KINGDOM), 1960

The Incredible String Band, 1967
(UNITED KINGDOM)

Norman Kennedy, 1966 (UNITED KINGDOM)

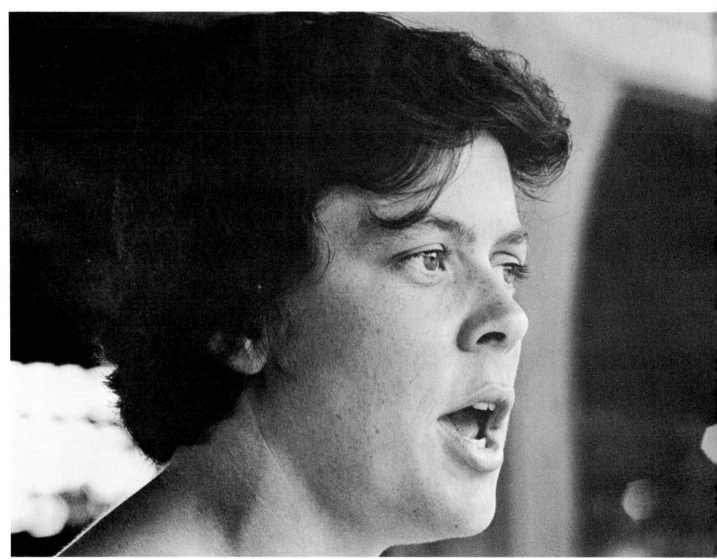

Jean Redpath, 1963 (UNITED KINGDOM)

334

London, 1968

Bob Davenport, 1967 (UNITED KINGDOM)

Seamus Ennis, 1964 (UNITED KINGDOM)

335

(left to right) Stefan Grossman, Maria Grossman, Ruth X, and Marc Silber, 1968

Lou Killen, 1966 (UNITED KINGDOM)

ft) Young Tradition, 1967 (UNITED KINGDOM)

Margaret Barry and Michael Gorman, 1965 (IRELAND)

A. L. Lloyd, 1965 (UNITED KINGDOM)

A. L. Loyd, Michael Gorman, and Margaret Barry, 1965 (UNITED KINGDOM and IRELAND)

Alan Mills, 1962 (CANADA)

resolved itself into one major point: After you have explored traditional music as far as you choose, what songs do you sing, what music do you write, what lyrics do you enunciate to express yourself?

To this question there were a score of answers. For a time, it looked as if the necessity to have one answer would just about destroy the folk movement. But the movement proved much hardier than that and has outlived the problematic phase of 1964–67. The answer to the big question was answered, if we may hazard an interpretation of their actions, in such manners as this:

PETE SEEGER: Tradition is still not fully explored and topical songs are a bottomless well. As long as life moves, music moves, as long as kids are crying, there will be lullabies written and sung.

Jean Carignan, 1962 (CANADA)

Alanis O'Bomsawin, 1962 (CANADA)

341

LEN CHANDLER: It's what's inside that counts, whether it's civil rights now or later, whether it's the problems of the Macdougal Street hippie or the man in the White House. Music and lyrics just come out as you feel them.

TOM PAXTON: The world is not all that we want, although there is much worth savoring. But tomorrow's newspaper is enough to make a man angry, enough to make him speak out, if not in anger, then to at least laugh the evil ones off the map.

PAT SKY: A little love, a little whimsy, a little W. C. Fields, and a little longing for the things we all dream about. Just life, man, just life.

BOB DYLAN: It's all music, no more, no less.

Helene Baillargeon, 1962 (CANADA)

Bonnie Dobson, 1965 (CANADA)

Tom Kines, 1962 (CANADA)

Stanley G. Triggs, 1962 (CANADA)

Karen James, 1962 (CANADA)

Gordon Lightfoot, Ian Tyson, Donovan, and Sylvia Tyson, 1965

Balfa Freres, (CAJUN) 1967

Gordon Lightfoot, 1965 (CANADA)

344

Bonnie Dobson, 1968 (CANADA)

The Beers Family, (UPPER NEW YORK STATE) 1966

Leonard Cohen, 1967 (CANADA)

Cape Breton Singers, 1965 (CANADA)

346

London, 1968

Tommy Makem, 1961 (IRELAND)

Joe Heany, 1966 (IRELAND)

Landreneau Band, (CAJUN) 1964

Pat Clancy, 1960 (IRELAND)

Joe Heaney and Liam Clancy, 1966 (IRELAND)

348

London, 1968

Clancy Brothers and Tommy Makem, 1964 (IRELAND)

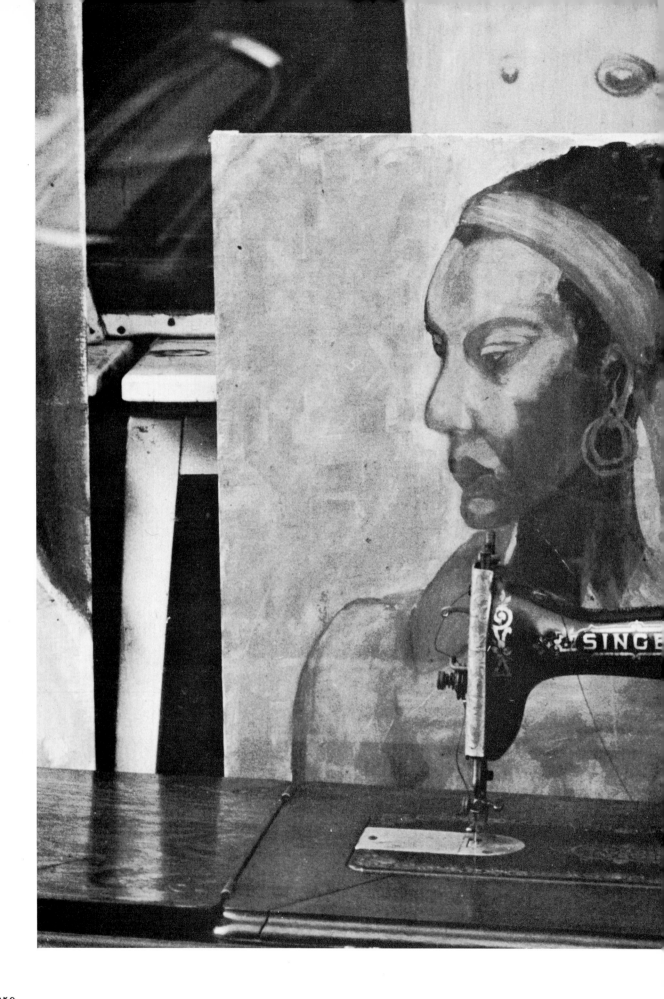

351

Ishangi Dance Troupe, 1965 (AFRICA)

Olatunji Dance Troupe, 1960 (AFRICA)

Spokes Mashiyane, 1965 (AFRICA)

Ishangi Dance Troupe, 1965 (AFRICA)

(Left) Inger LaFarge, 1965 (DENMARK),
(Right top) Hamza El Din (NORTH
AFRICA) 1965, *(Right bottom)* Sonia
Malkin, 1964 (FRANCE)

The last quote, no interpretation but a direct quote, is one answer to the problem that, for all its brevity, opens up the widest door. Dylan says there are no rules to break, only new doors to open, new ways to sing, new thoughts and feelings to explore. It's all music, no more, no less.

The multiplicity of answers will undoubtedly continue. While we have no single answer, we feel that one has to be a pluralist to maintain one's balance in a complex world. *Broadside, Little Sandy Review, Sing Out!, Crawdaddy,* and a dozen other magazines to develop out of the folk movement may not speak in accord, but let us hope they will move toward general areas of agreement. Music appreciation is a lot more valuable than the consistent depreciation that has characterized the folk press. Rules and rulers ought to be outlawed and freedom ought to be the only catechism.

Kiva American Indian Group, 1963

Henry Crowdog (AMERICAN INDIAN), 1968

Patrick Sky, 1968 (AMERICAN INDIAN)

Kiva American Indian Group, 1963

Buffy Sainte-Marie, 1966 (AMERICAN INDIAN)

Peter LaFarge, 1963 (AMERICAN INDIAN)

Schlomo Carlbach, 1964 (CHASSIDIC)

(Left) Moishe Bressler, 1967 (YIDDISH),
(Right top) Mark Oaf, 1958 (YIDDISH),
(Right bottom) Ruth Rubin, 1964
(YIDDISH)

INDEX

Abbott, O. J., 333
Abernathy, Rev. Dr. Ralph D., 185
Abrahams, Roger, 81
Abyssinian Baptist Chorus, 173
Acuff, Roy, 22, 210
Adderly, Cannonball, 173
Addiss, Steve, 359
Ain't You Got a Right to the Tree of Life? (Carawan), 185
Albany (Ga.), 179, 182, 184–185, 186
Albany Movement, The, 179
Alex Bradford's Gospel Group, 174–175
Almanac House, 103
Almanac Singers, The, 96, 98, 103
American Broadcasting Company, 132
American Songbag, The (Sandburg), 80
Americus (Ga.), 186
Andersen, Eric, 118, 259, 318, 319
Anderson, Casey, 128
Angie, Sally, 27, 330
Anglo-American Folksong Scholarship (Wilgus), 81
Angola (La.), 236
Animals, The, 256
Apollo Theater (New York), 178, 258
Appalachians, Southern, 42
Archive of American Folk Song, 247
Arhoolie (label), 240
Arlen, Harold, 231
Arnoldi, Paul, 270
Asch (label), 88
Asch, Moses ("Moe"), 47, 79, 84, 88, 143, 146
Asheville Folk Festivals, 43
Ashley, Clarence, 18, 55, 211
Ashley, Tom, 46
Atkins, Chet, 210
Avalon (Miss.), 50, 54
Axton, Hoyt, 128

Baedeaux, Ed, 79
Baez, Joan, vii, 2, 4, 6, 91, 120, 121, 122, 123, 192, 270, 272
Baillargeon, Helene, 341, 342
Baldwin, James, 49
Balfa Freres, 344
Barker, Horton, 45, 46, 52
"Barn Dance," 203
Barry, Margaret, (her hands) 30, 34, 292, 332, 338, 339
Bartók, Béla, 141
Battle (label), 173
Bayard, Samuel, 81, 88
Beatles, The, 8, 256, 259, 264, 270, 278
"Beatles Backlash, The," 264
Beck, Elder, 176
Beers, Fiddler Bob, 48, 99, 128
Beers Family, The, 345
Belafonte, Harry, 98, 104, 141, 288
Bellamy, Peter, 156, 316
Berline, Byron, 58, 217

Berline, Lue, 217
Berry, Chuck, 8, 258
Bibb, Leon, 118, 128
Biehusen, Thiele, (with Roy) 148
Bikel, Theodore ("Theo"), 80, 102, 128, 129, 130
Billboard magazine, 268
Birdland (night club), 176
Bitter End, The (café), 128
"Black Nativity," 173
Blakey, Art, 141
Bloomfield, Mike, 263
Blue, David, 270, 324
Blue Grass Boys, 213, 218
Blues Band, The, 238
Blues Fell This Morning, (Oliver), 232
Blue Sky Boys, The, 210
Blues Project, The, 10, 254, 270, 280–281
Bluesville record series (Prestige), 240
Boggs, Dock, 60, 219
Born to Win (Guthrie), 96
Borum, Memphis Willie, 49, 236, 239
Bound for Glory (Guthrie), 96
Boyd, Eddie, 243
Bradford, Alex, 173, 174–175
Brand, Oscar, 91, 102, 103, 297
Branford (Conn.), 132
Bread and Puppet Theater, 298
Bressler, Moishe, 365
Britain (*see also* England), 249, 252, 256–57
"British Invasion," 257, 259
Broadside magazine, 356, 360
Bronson, Prof. Bertrand, 76
Brooklyn (N.Y.) (*see also* New York), 196–197, 234
Brooks, Harvey, 259
Brooks, John Benson, 141
Broonzy, Big Bill, 47, 60, 90–91, 234, 258
Brothers Four, The, 113
Brown, Mrs. Pearly, 172, 185
Brown, Rev. Pearly, 172, 185
Browne, Jackson, 260, 277
Brownsville (Brooklyn), 234
Brubeck, Dave, 141
Buckley, Tim, 279, 323
Bull, Sandy, 6, 128, 276
Burke, John, 209
Butterfield, Paul, 263, 268
Byrds, The, 268

Cadwell, Paul, 48, 85
Cage, Butch, 45
Cajun Band (*see also* Landreneau Cajun Band), 17, 29, 32
Cajuns, 302
Cameron, Isla, 289
Camilla (Ga.), 186
Camp, Hamilton, 158
Campbell, Archie, 210

Campbell, Lucie, 178
Camp Creek Boys, *see* Galax String Band
"Candy Man," 54
Cannon, Gus, 49, 239
Cape Breton Singers, 7, 183, 346
Caravans, The, 173
Carawan, Candy, 185
"Car, Car," 94
Carawan, Guy, 287, (and son) 140, 185, 191, 194
Carignan, Jean, 294, 297, 341
Carlbach, Sclomo, 364
Carlisle, Cliff, 213
Carlton, Gaither, 51, 208
Carnegie Hall, 104, 240
Carpenter, French, 223
Carr, Leroy, 234
Carson, Fiddling John, 204
Carter, Maybelle, 46, 48, 137, 218, 219
Carter, Sara, 48, 218, 222
Carter Family, Original, *see* Original Carter Family
Carter Family, The, 94
Cash, Johnny, 210, 215, 220, 301, 361
Chad Mitchell Trio, The, 113, 293
Chambers Brothers, 177, 242
Chambers Dancers, The, 244
Chandler, Len, 191, 342
Chang Ming Quang Group, 359
Charles, Ray, 173
Charles River Valley Boys, The, 217, 220
Charlotte (N.C.), 186
Charters, Sam, 49, 81, 258
Chicago, 113, 247, 258, 264
Child, Prof. Francis James (*see also* Child ballads), 74–76
Child, Marilyn, 100
Child ballads (*see also* Child, Prof. Francis James), 4, 74–76
Clancy, Liam (*see also* Clancy Brothers, The), 292, 348
Clancy, Pat (*see also* Clancy Brothers, The), 292, 348
Clancy, Tom (*see also* Clancy Brothers, The), 238, 292
Clancy Brothers, The (*see also* Clancy, Liam; Clancy, Pat; Clancy, Tom), 292, 349
Clancy-Makem quartet, 292
Clara Ward Singers, The, 173, 176
Clark, Dave, *see* Dave Clark Five, The
Clayton, Paul, 100
Clements, Zeke, 210
Cleveland, James, 173
Club 47, 128
Cohen, John, 46, 160, 217
Cohen, Leonard, 321, 345
Collins, Judy, 2, 128, 129, 134, 262
Congress of Racial Equality (CORE), 186
Coon Creek Girls, 214
Cooney, Michael, 19

Cooper, Clarence, 98, 156
Cooper, Stoney, 207
Copland, Aaron, 141
CORE, see Congress of Racial
   Equality
Cottell, Jenes, 223
Cotton, Elizabeth, 6, 62, 66–67
Country Gentlemen, 217
Country Music Story, The
   (Shelton and Goldblatt), 207
Cousin Emmy, 210, 211, 217
Country Joe and the Fish, 253
Crawdaddy magazine, 356
Crofut, Bill, 359
Crowdog, Henry, 362
Cumberland Mountains (Ky.), 50, 77
Current, Gloster B., 184

D'Amato, Maria, 60, 149, 266
Dane, Barbara, 92, 100, 238
Darling, Eric, 95, 100, 104
Dave Clark Five, The, 256
Davenport, Bob, 18, 289, 293, 335
Davis, Mrs. Gary, 238
Davis, Rev. Gary, 58, (his living room)
   68, 71, 186, 234, 238
Dawson (Ga.), 186
Delmark (label), 240
Din, Hamza El, 355
Disc (label), 88
Distler, Marion, 92
Dixie Hummingbirds, The, 170–171,
   177, 186
Dixon, Dorsey, 51
Dixon, Willie, 65, 236, 242–243
Dixon Brothers, The, 88
Dobson, Bonnie, 128, 137, 342, 345
Donovan, 120, 155, 250–251, 256,
   289, 344
Dorsey, Thomas A. ("Georgia Tom"),
   178
Dorson, Richard, 81
Down Beat magazine, 173
Driftwood, Jimmy, 3, (and son)
   208, 223
Drinkard Singers, The, 173
Dubliners, The, 292
Dudley, Dave, 209
Durham (N.C.), 179
Duy, Pham, 359
Dyer–Bennet, Richard, 91, 117
Dylan, Bob, 5, 6, 8, 121, 122, 124, 125,
   192, 256–257, 259, 264, 268, 295, 323,
   342, 356

Eaglin, Blind Snooks, 236
Electra (label), 42
Elliott, Cass, 271
Elliott, Jack, 2, 4, 113, 135, 205, 322
Emmy, Cousin, see Cousin Emmy
England (see also Britain), 249, 256,
   257
English, Logan, 119, 128
English and Scottish Popular
   Ballads, The (Child), 74–76

Ennis, Seamus, 17, 335
Eskin, Sam, 100
Estes, Sleepy John, 51, 62, 232, 234, 235
Ethnic Folkways Library, 289
Europe, Western, 258
Everly Brothers, The, 256

Fahey, John, 158
Faier, Billy, (his water bag) 68, 93, 113
Fariña, Mimi, 15, 136, 272, 273
Fariña, Richard, 15, 269, 272, 309, 324
Farrell, Eileen, 231
Feliciano, José, 127
Fikes, Bettie Mae, 187, 191
Fish, Country Joe and the, 253
Five Blind Boys, The, 173
Flanders, Margaret, 81
Flatt, Lester, 215, 218
Foggy Mountain Boys, The, 218
Folk City, Gerdes', 128
Folk-Legacy (label), 42
Folklore Center, 142
Folk-Lyric (label), 42
Folkways (label), 42, 88, 91, 92
Fox, Manny, 10
Franklin, Aretha, 173, 180–181
Franklin, Rev. C. L., 176
Freedom Singers, The, 190, 191,
   193, 194
"Freewheeling Bob Dylan, The"
   (album), 264
Friends of Old-Time Music, The,
   46, 224, 226
Fugs, The, 254, 255, 264–265
Fuller, Jesse, 235, 237

Gagnier, Sean, 29
Gahr, David, 2, 5
Galax (Va.), 43
Galax String Band (or Camp Creek
   Boys), 217
Garfunkel, see Simon and Garfunkel
Garland, Jim, 57, 88
Gaslight, The (café), 6, 128
Gate of Horn, The, 128
Gaugin, 42
Gauthier, Claude, 297
Geer, Will, 94, 102
Georgia Council on Human
   Relations, 186
Georgia Sea Island Singers, 52, 55,
   177, 185, 194
Gerdes' Folk City, 128
Gibson, Bob, 93, 113
Gilbert, Ollie, 59, 223
Gilbert, Ronnie, 95, 103
Glazer, Joe, 91
Glazer, Tom, 91
"Gloryland March," 207
Glover, Tony, (his boots) 223,
   269, 274, 275
"Go down, Kennedy," 182
"Go down, Moses," 182
Goldstein, Kenneth, 81, 91

Good, Hally, 103
Gooding, Cynthia, 91, 113
"Goodnight, Irene," 91, 103
Gorman, Michael, 34, 224, 332,
   338, 339
Gospel Harmonettes, The,
   170–171, 179
Gospel Pearls, The, 173
Grandison Singers, The, 173, 176
"Grand Ole Opry," 49–50, 203–206
Grandpa Jones, 204, 210
Graves, Buck, 216
Great Britain, see Britain; England
Green, Archie, 8, 81
Green, Debbie, 118
Greenbriar Boys, The, 43, 117, 206, 220
Greenhill, Mitch, 126
Greenhill, Mrs. Mitch, 4
Greenway, John, 81
Greenwich Village (see also Washing-
   ton Square Park), 46, 103, 117, 264
Grossman, Albert, 256
Grossman, Maria, 337
Grossman, Stefan, 260, 330, 337
Guard, Dave, 108
Guest, Roy, 289
Gunning, Sarah, 8, 46
Guthrie, Arlo, 156, 299, 326
Guthrie, Woody, 91, 94, 96, 103,
   (his fiddle) 104, (and family)
   104–105, 132
Guy, Buddy, 20
gypsy girl, a, 278

Haley, Bill, 252
Hall, Juanita, 241
Hamer, Fannie Lou, 33, 191, 300, 301
Hamilton, Frank, 102, 104
Hammond, John, 155, 269, 271
"Happy With the Blues," 231
Hardin, Tim, 258, 259, 269, 320
Hardon, Ben, 209
Harlem, 188–189
Harris, Emmy Lou, 163, 209
Hart County Chapter, NAACP, 183
Hartford, John, 16
Hartwell (Ga.), 183
Harvesters, The, 145
Havens, Richie, 116, 175
"Have you ever been mistreated?" 240
Hawes, Bess, 100
Hawes, Butch, 103
Hay, George D., 203
Hays, Lee, 94, 103
Heany, Joe, 347, 348
Hellerman, Fred, 80, 95, 103
Herald, John, 117
Hester, Carolyn, 115, 128, 134, 164, 317
Hickok, Elgia, 52
Highlander Folk School, 185
Highwaymen, The, 113
Highway Q.C.'s, The, 173
Hill, Joe, 88
Hinton, Sam, 105
Holcomb, Roscoe, 7, 46, 48, 55, 101

Holmes, Rev. Oliver W., 186
Holt, Will, 105
Holzman, Jac, 80
Homer and Jethro, 210
Hooker, John Lee, 47, 236, 241
Hootenanny (magazines), 137
"Hootenanny" (TV show), 132–137
Hopkins, Sam ("Lightning"),
    234, 240, 248
Horton, Zilphia, 185
Hoskins, Tom, 54
House, Son, 58, 247, 271
Houston, Cisco, 101, 103
Howling Wolf, 185, 242, 258
Hudak, Mike, 209
Hughes, Langston, 100, 173, 178
hungry i, the, 128
Hurt, Mississippi John, ii, 2, 4, 50–58,
    51, 62, 236, 241

Ian and Sylvia (*see also* Tyson, Ian;
    Tyson, Sylvia), 128, 144, 244, 292
Ian, Janis, 26, 268, 327
Ice House, The (coffeehouse), 128
"I Gave My Love a Cherry," 3, 286
"I'll Overcome, Someday," 185
Incredible String Band, The, 333
Indian Neck (Conn.), 132
Inquisition, The (coffeehouse), 128
Irish Rovers, The, 292
Ishangi Dance Troupe, 288, 352, 354
"I've Got a Right to Sing the Blues,"
    231
Ives, Burl, 88, 90

Jackson, Aunt Molly, 88
Jackson, Bruce, 79
Jackson, Mahalia, 172–173, 176
James, Karen, 341, 343
James, Skip, 6, 51, 53, 57, 62, 236, 244
James, Son, 236
James, Dr. Willis, 52, 88, 174
Jansch, Bert, 331, 332
Jean, *see* Jim and Jean
Jeanie, *see* Sandie and Jeanie
Jefferson, Blind Lemon, 234
Jethro, *see* Homer and Jethro
Jim and Jean, 128
Jim Kweskin Jug Band, 267, 269
John Edwards Memorial Foundation,
    220
Johnson, Bernice, 184, 190, 194, 195
Johnson, Lonnie, 236
Johnson, Robert, 236
Jones, Bessie, 52, 54, 55, 185, 194, 195
Jones, Bob, 126
Jones, Charles, 179
Jones, Eva Thompson, 203
Jones, George, 210
Jones, Grandpa, *see* Grandpa Jones
Jones, Mrs., 204
Joplin, Janis, 6
Jordan, Vernon E., Jr., 183–184

Kalvik, Finn, 331

Kathy and Carol, 155
Katz, Fred, 141
Kazee, Buell, 20
Keith, Bill, 217
Kennedy, Norman, 289, 332, 333
Kentucky Colonels, The, 214
Kerouac, Jack, 40
Kessinger, Clark, 47
Killen, Lou, 289, 337
Kim Loy Wong, 119
Kindred, Lisa, 128
Kines, Tom, 341, 343
King, B. B., 18, 258
King, Rev. Dr. Martin Luther, Jr.,
    179, 185, 186
"King of the Road," 213
Kingston Trio, The, 104, 108–111, 113
Kirkpatrick, Rev. Frederick, 21
"Kisses Sweeter Than Wine," 103
Kiva American Indian Group,
    362, 363
Kodály, Zoltán, 141
Koerner, John, 269, 274, 315
Koester, Bob, 259
Kooper, Al, 271
Kraber, Tony, 92
Krause, Bernie, 104, 126
Kunstadt, Len, 259
Kupferberg, Tuli, 260
Kweskin, Jim (*see also* Jim Kweskin
    Jug Band), 267, (with family) 268
Kweskin, Marilyn, (and daughter)
    127, 268

LaFarge, Inger, 355
LaFarge, Peter, 134, 301, 306–307,
    326, 363
Lampell, Millard, 94, 103
Landreneau Cajun Band
    (*see also* Cajun Band), 348
Langstaff, John, 91
Lay, Sam, 263
Leach, MacEdward, 81
Leadbelly (Huddie Ledbetter), 91, 236
Ledbetter, Huddie, *see* Leadbelly
Lee, Bill, 239
Lee, Wilma, 207
Lees, Gene, 138
Leonda, 237
Lester, Julius, (and daughter) 127,
    302–303, 317
Leventhal, Harold, 80, 103–104
Lewis, Furry, 49, 236, 239
Lewis, George, 246
Leyrac, Monique, 297
Library of Congress, 91, 247, 271
Lightfoot, Gordon, (his guitar) 12,
    32, 322, 344
Lilly Brothers, 207
Limeliters, The, 10, 113
Lipscomb, Mance, 47, 236
Little Richard, 256, 259
Little Sandy Review (magazine), 356
Liverpool (*see also* Britain; England),
    256

Lloyd, A. L., 22, 34, 52, 88, 146,
    289, 332, 338, 339
Lomax, Alan, 14, 76–77, 81, 88, 94, 143
Lomax, John A., 42, 76–77
Lomaxes, The (*see also* Lomax, Alan;
    Lomax, John A.), 91
Los Angeles, *see* Sunset Strip
Louisiana State Prison, 236
Love, Dorothy, 170, 179, 183
Lovin' Spoonful, The, 261, 268
Lukeman, Alex, 134
Lunsford, Bascolm Lamar, 43
Lyman, Mel, 267

McAdoo, Bill, 116, 304
McAllester, Prof. David, 301
McCarthyism, 40, 103, 128
MacColl, Ewan, 289-290, 333
McCurdy, Ed, 100, 104, 110
McDowell, Fred, 63, 236, 245
McGee, Kirk, 47, 49, 58, 214–215
McGee, Sam, 45, 47, 49, 58, 208,
    214–215
McGhee, Brownie, 47, 91,
    (and daughter) 99, 234, 236
McGuire, Barry, 268
McMichen, "Pappy," 207-208, 211
McReynolds, Jessie, 206
McReynolds, Jim, 206
Mahler, Gustav, 141
Makeba, Miriam, 288
Makem, Tommy, 292, 347, 349
Malkin, Sonia, 355
Manes, Almon, 205
Manes, Virginia, 205
Manhattan, *see* New York
Mann, Herbie, 141
Marais and Miranda, 91, 288
Marrs, Ernie, 99
Martin, Roberta, *see* Roberta Martin
    Singers, The
Mashiyane, Spokes, 288, 353
Memphis Slim, 65, 232, 236
Memphis Willie B., *see* Borum,
    Memphis Willie
Michaux, Elder Solomon Lightfoot,
    176
"Midnight Special," 91
Miles, Long John, 119
Miller, Roger, 210, 213
Mills, Alan, 292, 340, 341
Miranda, *see* Marais and Miranda
Mississippi Delta, 50, 53, 247
Mississippi John, *see* Hurt,
    Mississippi John
Mississippi State Prison, 186
Mitchell, Chad (*see also* Chad Mitchell
    Trio), 293
Mitchell, Joni, 147, 321
Monroe, Bill, 2, 46, 212, 213, 218
Montgomery, Little Brother, 235
Morganfield, Mackinley,
    see Muddy Waters
Morris Brothers, 205
Mothers of Invention, 282–283

Mounteagle (Tenn.), 185
Mount Zion Baptist Church, 184–185
Moving Star Hall Singers, 56–57, 171, 184
Muddy Waters (Mackinlay Morgenfield), 238, 246, 247, 256
Muldaur, Geoff, 268
Murdoch, Bruce, 29, 160, 324

NAACP, see National Association for the Advancement of Colored People
Nashville (Tenn.), 50, 200, 201, 202, 203, 204, 210, 224
Nashville–Davidson County district, 202
National Association for the Advancement of Colored People (NAACP), 183
Native Son (Wright), 232
Neil, Fred, 269
Nelson, Paul, 25, 81, 270
New England Dance Society, 1959, 10
New Lost City Ramblers, The, 209, 226
Newport (R.I.), 302
Newport Children's Folk Festival, 1966, 9, 32
Newport Folk Festivals, 6, 46, 54, 101, 130, 132, 183, 209, 235, 288, 302; 1959, 110; 1960, 130; 1963, 12; 1964, 1, 27, 28, 30–31, 55, 194; 1965, 5, 14, 22, 27, 88; 1966, 11, 16–17, 18–19, 23, 24–25, 33, 86, 136, 207, 208, 209, 246
Newport Folk Foundation, 25, 51, 224, 302
New World Singers, The, 297
New York (see also Brooklyn; Carnegie Hall; Greenwich Village; Harlem; Washington Square Park), 178, 196–197, 224, 258
New York Folk Festival, The, 8, 10, 160
New York Ramblers, 209
New York Times, The, survey by, 179
New York University, 46
Nicolle, Arthur, 34, 332
Niles, John Jacob, 91, 93, 100
Nixon, Hammy, 51
Noonan, Steve, 260, 327
Nubin, Katy Bell, 1, 77
Nye, Hermes, 91

Oaf, Mark, 365
Oberstein, Eli, 84
O'Bomsawin, Alanis, 341
Ochs, Phil, 128, 140, 305, 318, 319
Odetta, 113, 154, 178, 190
Ohrlin, Glenn, 29, 205.
Okeh Records, 54
Olatunji Dance Troupe, 353
Older, Larry, 48, 211
"Old Pritchett," see Pritchett, Laurie
Oliver, Paul, 232
Onward Brass Band, 33
"Opry," see Grand Ole Opry

Orchestra Hall (Chicago), 113
Original Carter Family, 84
Oster, Harry, 45, 81
"Over my head I see freedom . . .," 184
Owens, Buck, 210

Paine, Ed, 248
Paley, Tom, 102, 160
Parchman (Miss.), 186
Paris, 231
Parker, Chet, 208
Parsons, Phoeba, 217, 223
Parsons, Roscoe, 223
"Pastures of Plenty," 94
Paton, Caroline, 140
Paton, Sandy, 52, 140
Patterson, Joe, 59
Paul Butterfield Blues Band, 263, 264
Paxton, Tom, 116, 294, 304, 318, 319, 342
Peacock (label), 173
Pearl, Cousin Minnie, 210
Peer, Ralph, 84, 210
Pennywhistlers, The, 137
Pentangle, The, 331
"People, if you hear me humming . . .," 230
People's Songs, 101
Pepper's Lounge (Chicago), 258
Perkins, Carl, 252
Peter, Paul and Mary (see also Travers, Mary), 91, 113, 130–131, 192
Phillips, Guy, 209
Phipps Family, The, 216
Pierce, Billie, 246
Preservation Hall Band, 246
Presley, Elvis, 252
Prestige (label), 42, 240
Price, Sammy, 173
Pritchett, Laurie, Chief of Police ("Old Pritchett"), 182, 185–186
Proffitt, Frank, 49, 65, 110
Purple Onion, The, 128

Rachel, Yank, 51, 62
Ramsey, Fred, 81
Randolph, Vance, 80
Ray, Dave, 269, 274, 275, 314–315
Reagon, Cordell, 190
Redpath, Jean, 289, 334
Reed, Susan, 91
Reese, Della, 173
Reese, Doc, 52, 62
Reeves, Goebel (see also Texas Drifter, The), 220
Reisner, Bob, 138, 141
Reno, Don, 207
Reynolds, Malvina, 310, 326
Reynolds, Nick, 108
Rice, Midge, 215
Riddle, Almeda, 45, 46, 49, (her hands) 58
Rinzler, Ralph, 6–8, 46, 163, 213
Ritchie, Jean, 17, 50, 101, 110–111, (her hands) 224

Ritchie Family, The, 50, 77
Riverside (label), 42
Roberta Martin Singers, The, 173
Roberts, Kenny, 207
Roberts, Robin, 91
Robertson, Eck, 48, 58, 207, 208
Robeson, Paul, 91
Robinson, Earl, 81, 91
Rock Hill (S.C.), 186
Roderick, Judy, 137, 245
Rodgers, Jimmie, 84, 210, 213
Rodriguez Brothers, The, 64, 237
Rogers, Grant, 49
Rolling Stones, The, 252, 256
Rooftop Singers, The, 113, 118
Rooney, Jim, 217
Roosevelt, Franklin D., 90, 203
Rothschild, Charles, 43
Rousseau, Jean Jacques, 42
Rubin, Ruth, 365
Rush, Tom, 163, 326
Ruth X, 337

Sacred Harp Singers, 55, 182
Sadler, Sgt. Barry, 296
Sainte-Marie, Buffy, 3, 114, 292, 301, 320, 363
"Salty Dog," 54
Sandburg, Carl, 77, 80
Sandie and Jeanie, 118
San Francisco, 264
Satherley, Art, 84
Savoy (label), 173
Scarborough, Dorothy, 80–81
Schlamme, Martha, 100, 102
Schubert, Franz, 141
Schumann, Peter, 298
Scruggs, Earl, 215, 218, 220
Sea Islands (Ga.; S.C.), (see also Georgia Sea Island Singers), 194, 302
Sebastian, John, 270, 271
Sebastian, Lorey, 270, 271
Second Fret (café), 128
Seeger, Charles, 55, 80, 88
Seeger, Constance, 55, 85
Seeger, Mike, 7, 46, 55, (and sons) 89, 213, 216, 217, 219, 294
Seeger, Peggy, 87, 333
Seeger, Pete, 6, 9, 10, 27, 43, 80, 82–83, (and daughter) 84, 85, (and family) 85, 86, 87, (Seeger cabin) 90, 94, 96, 98, 101, 102, 103, 104, 111, 130, 132–134, 137, 154, 185, 193, 270, 294, 295, 297, 341
Seeger, Tinya, 84
Seeger, Toshi, 27, 80
Sellers, Brother John, 174, 235
Settle, Mike, 119, 294, 301
Shane, Bob, 108.
Sharp, Cecil, 42, 77
Shelton, Robert, 57, 103, 137, 207
Shepherd, Dewey, 205, 208
Shepherd, Jean, 138
Shostakovich, Dimitri, 141
Silber, Irwin, 10, 79, 146

Silber, Marc, 81, 290, 337
Silver, Horace, 174
Silverman, Jerry, 145
Simon and Garfunkel, 268, 325
Sing Out! magazine, 101, 146, 356, 360
Skillet Lickers, The, 218
Sky, Patrick, 301, 311, 323, 342, 362
Sloan, P. F., 268
Smith, Arthur, 214-215
Smith, Carrie, 173
Smith, Dan, 35
Smith, Harry, 99, 101
Smith, Hobart, 44, 49
Smith, Jimmy, 174
Smith, Oliver, 210
Smither, Chris, 139
SNCC ("SNICK"), *see* Student
    Non-Violent Coordinating
    Committee
Snow, Hank, 213
Snow, Jim, 209
Snow, Kirby, 47, 202
Solomon, Linda, 17, 137
Solomon, Maynard, 80
Solomon of the Kaleidoscope, 20
"So Long, It's Been Good to
    Know You," 94
Sorrels, Rosalie, 208
Soul-Stirrers, The, 173
Southern Christian Leadership
    Conference, 179
Southern Fife and Drum Corps
    (*see also* Young, Ed), 187, 194, 235
Southern Regional Council, 186
Spann, Otis, 238
Spence, Joseph, 6
Spivey, Victoria, 236
Spoelstra, Kathy, 140
Spoelstra, Mark, 140, 308
Sprung, Roger, 117, 208
Stanley Brothers, The, 46, 183, 206
Staples, Mavis, 175
Staple Singers, The, 6, 173, 179,
    195, 238
Stars of Faith, The, 173
Stearns, Marshal, 100
Stekert, Ellen, 81
Stevens Singers, The, 173
Stinson (label), 88
Stookey, Paul, 130
Stringbean, 207
Student Non-Violent Coordinating
    Committee (SNCC; "SNICK"),
    179, 190, 195, 291
Sunset Strip (Los Angeles), 264
Swan Silvertones, The, 170–171, 173
Swarthmore College, 132
Sweet Chariot, The (night club), 176
Sykes, Roosevelt, 236
Sylvia, *see* Ian and Sylvia

Tabernacle (label), 173
Tabernacle Singers, 173
Taj Mahal, 25
Takimi, Saz, 358

Tampa Red, 236
Tanner, Gid, 218
Tarlton, Jimmie, 52, 219
Tarriers, The, 113, 140
Teatro Campesino, 298
Ten O'Clock Scholar, The (café), 128
Terry, Sonny, 47, 91, 93, 236
Testament (label), 247
Texas Drifter, The,
    see Reeves, Goebel
Texas Work Song Group, 195
Thacher, Bill, 296
Tharpe, Sister Rosetta, 174, 177
"This Land Is Your Land," 94
Thomas, Willie, 45
Thompson, Uncle Jimmy, 203
Timmons, Bobby, 174
Tindley, C. Albert, 178
"Tom Dooley," 49, 110
Tracy, Andrew, 358
Tracy, Paul, 358
Traum, Artie, 117
Traum, Happy, 157
Travers, Mary (*see also* Peter, Paul
    and Mary), 22, (her feet) 29,
    132–133, 233, 256
Travis, Merle, 60, 207
Triana, Chinin de, 357
Triggs, Stanley G., 341, 343
True Vine Singers, The, 179
Tubb, Ernest, 210, 213
Tyson, Ian (*see also* Ian and Sylvia),
    322, 344
Tyson, Sylvia (*see also* Ian and Sylvia),
    32, (her hands) 224, 323, 344

UCLA, *see* University of California
    at Los Angeles
Union Grove (N.C.), 6, 43
Union Grove Fiddlers' Convention,
    43, 46
University of California at Berkeley,
    75-76, 132
University of California at Los
    Angeles, 132, 220
University of Chicago, 6, 132
University Settlement Steel Band, 119

Van Doer, Beth, 136
Van Ronk, Dave, 113, 254
Viking Hotel, 6
Village, The, *see* Greenwich Village
Village Gate, The, 128, 240
Village Vanguard, 103
Village Voice, The, 138
Von Schmidt, Eric, 245
Von Schmidts Family, The, 115, 136

Wakeley, Jimmy, 210
Wakeley, Lance, 276
Walker, Frank, 84
Walker, Jerry Jeff, 317
Walker, Peter, 276
Wallace, Henry, 103
Wallace, Sippie, 249

Walters, Annie, 34, 332
Ward, Clara (*see also* Clara Ward
    Singers, The), 176
Warner, Frank, 97, 110
Warrenton (Va.), 43
Warwick, Dionne, 173
Washington, Ernestine, 173
Washington, Jackie, 162
Washington Square Park (New York),
    117
Watson, Arnold, 51
Watson, Doc, 46, 51, 61, 137, 206
Watson, Mrs. General Dixon, 59
Watson, Merle, 61
Watson, Ora, 216
Watson Family, The, 183
Weavers, The, 96, 98, 103–104, 113
Wein, George, 130
Weissberg, Eric, 117, 160
Welding, Pete, 247
Wells, Junior, 20, 258
"We Shall Overcome," 185
We Shall Overcome (Carawan), 185
West, Harry, 91
West, Hedy, 114
West, Jeannie, 91
"When the King Comes Marching
    In," 186
"When the Saints Go Marching
    In," 186
White, Bukka, 56, 185, 236, 241
White, Josh, 90, 91, 236, 258
White, Newman Ivey, 80
Whitman, Walt, 77
Wilgus, D. K., 81
Wilkens, Rev. Robert, 51, 57, 175
Williams, Big Joe, 57,
    (his hands) 58, 65, 236, 242
Williams, Hank, 210, 220
Williams, Marion, 173
Williams, Robert Pete, 44, 236, 237
Williams, Vaughan, 141
Williamson, Sonny Boy, II, 236
Wilson, Dave, 25
Wiseman, Mac, 214
"With God on Our Side," 6
WLS (radio station), 203
Wong, Kim Loy, 119
Wood, Hally, 91, 104
Woods, Maceo, 173
Wordsworth, William, 41–42
Wright, Richard, 232
WSM (radio station), 203

X, Ruth, 337

Yarrow, Peter, 130
Yellin, Bob (*see also* Greenbriar
    Boys, The), 43, 44, 46
Yomo Toro Group, 136
"You know, them rats is mean . . .," 232
Young, Ed, 187, 194, 235
Young, Israel ("Izzy"), 10, 79, 106–107
Young Brothers, The, 195
Young Tradition, 316, 336